The Anatomy of Time

An Introduction to the Living Time Perspective

J.W. Pressler

YJ Press Publishing

Contents

Dedication

This book is dedicated to two souls

who share the same birthday.

To my father, Daniel Pressler — whose passing set me on a path of questioning time, existence, and the unseen currents of life.

And to my pug, Soho — whose passing left me wishing I could turn time back for just one more day.

This work offers the world a perspective that allows your paths to meet in time.

It was first published on your birthday, in celebration of the gift you both gave me.

Chapter One

Author's Introduction

Before we begin, I want to be clear about who I am — and perhaps more importantly, who I am not.

I did not earn a degree in philosophy. My formal studies were in criminal justice and psychology. But long before I stepped into a classroom, I was already asking the kinds of questions philosophers spend their lives circling.

Not by profession — but by nature.

We all arrive in the world with needs that ask something of life. Food, water, shelter — these are shared. But beneath them live quieter needs, less visible and far more personal.

One of mine has always been *logic*.

Not logic as a discipline, but logic as necessity. If something did not make sense to me, my mind searched for how it fit — sometimes patiently, sometimes relentlessly.

I needed to understand how things related to one another, and what role they played within the larger pattern of being alive.

Curiosity, I have come to believe, is itself a thread — one that appears in many lives in different forms, yet touches the same deeper structure.

You can often recognize it early in a child: the one who takes things apart simply to see how they work. That curiosity often reaches outward — into objects, systems, mechanisms.

Mine turned inward.

I never disassembled a radio. But I have taken emotion apart piece by piece, asking a different kind of question:

Why are you here?

Questions like this have followed me through life. Not as judgment. Not as resistance. But as an attempt to understand how experience functions — what each feeling, each moment, each disruption contributes to the larger weave of life.

My earliest clear memory of this need being activated came when I was five years old, standing in a moment no child should ever have to witness: watching my father pass away.

I have memories from before that — flickers, impressions — but they behave like smoke. The moment I try to hold them, they dissolve.

That moment did not simply fracture my childhood.

It fractured my understanding of the world.

Something had happened that demanded explanation, and none of the ones offered to me could carry its weight. That was the first time my curiosity turned fully inward — not toward answers, but toward meaning itself.

I did not have the language for it then, but the questions arrived immediately.

If people go to heaven, why not animals?

Why not the grass?

Why not everything that lives?

If man was created in God's image, why do we all look so different?

Why would one form of life matter more than another?

I did not know these were philosophical questions.

I only knew they were mine.

From that point forward, I found myself misaligned with institutional religion — not out of rebellion, but out of honesty. The explanations I was given did not correspond with what I observed in the world around me.

I was fortunate in a very important way. I had a mother who allowed me, even at that young age, the freedom to step away from the Church — not into certainty, but into inquiry. She trusted me to seek my own understanding, wherever it might lead.

Looking back now, I suspect my father's passing raised similar questions in her as well. The Mormon Church would return to our home later in life; while it was never the place for my beliefs, I remain grateful for the lens it offered. It became part of my unfolding.

These early experiences did not give me answers.

They gave me the next set of questions.

I carried them quietly through childhood, often without language to express what I was sensing. Much of this journey unfolded in private — through reflection, observation, and an ongoing attempt to understand how meaning, mystery, and structure coexist.

When I did try to share these thoughts, I was often misunderstood — not because others failed to listen, but because I had not yet learned how to translate what I perceived inwardly.

This journey was never entirely solitary. Over the years, I have been shaped by countless conversations — some brief, some enduring — that challenged me, grounded me, and expanded my way of seeing. Long before I had words for what I was exploring, there were people willing to listen, to question alongside me, and to offer their own hard-earned insight.

Experience, I have learned, is difficult to capture in words.

Some truths live in sensation, intuition, and awareness long before they find vocabulary.

Language cannot fully contain them. Metaphors help, but they are only bridges. Similes help, but they are only shadows. Analogy may balance the two, but it still falls short.

Writing is a tool — a useful one — but a limited one.

Look at any work from history. Each was shaped by its time, its culture, its audience. Separated by centuries, those same works often require interpretation. Even sacred texts are not immune to this — perhaps especially sacred texts.

Words evolve.

People evolve.

Perspective evolves.

And understanding must evolve with them.

But there is something easily forgotten in this process.

Every ancient text was once written in the *Now.*

Not in abstraction.

Not in hindsight.

In a living present moment — shaped by breath, body, fear, wonder, and attention — just as this one is.

The truth they point toward has not aged.

Only the language has.

Which means those texts are not the sole carriers of wisdom — they are records of encounters with it. The same reality they observed remains available, not because it was preserved in words, but because it continues to unfold in experience.

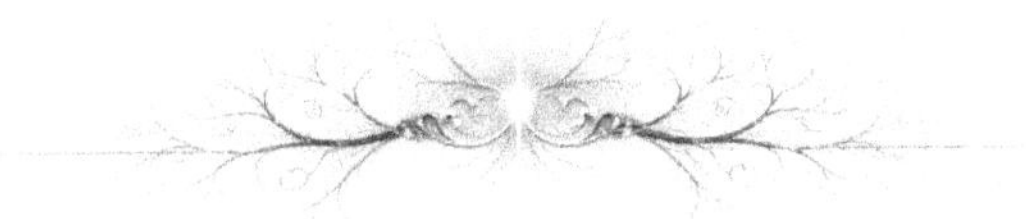

This perspective explores time — and time is a peculiar thing. One truth about time is that meaning itself changes. Even weeks or months from now, the meaning of these pages will have shifted. A hundred years from now, if someone were to encounter this work, it would still hold meaning — but not the same meaning that I had intended.

That is not a weakness.

It is a feature of living truth.

This model of understanding is not an attempt to prove or disprove anything.

It is not a doctrine.

It is not a declaration of truth.

It offers a place to stand and see time from a new perspective — a lens through which experience can be viewed differently.

What I offer here are not answers, but threads — threads of thought, observation, metaphor, and possibility.

Truth, as we experience it, is always shaped by vantage point. Change the perspective, and the truth shifts with it.

What follows is an invitation to notice patterns — not to accept conclusions. To soften assumptions, awaken curiosity, and allow questions back into the conversation.

Nothing more.

Nothing less.

I offer these pages as threads.

The tapestry — as always — belongs to you.

Chapter Two

The Limits and Power of Language

Human beings navigate life with a tool both magnificent and flawed: *language.*

While open to debate, language can be considered among the first technologies we created — evolving from simple sounds into complex words, symbols, and dialogue. It is the tool we use to shape the world inside our minds, and the bridge we use to carry those inner worlds into shared meaning and future thought.

But before we move further, we must acknowledge something essential:

Language is both our greatest instrument of understanding and our greatest barrier to it.

Words can express ideas, but they cannot be them.

They can point toward experience, but they can never fully contain it.

Try describing a sunset to someone born without sight.

Try explaining freedom to someone who has only known confinement.

Try offering a perfect definition of love, or joy, or grief.

Even something as simple as color resists certainty. We cannot know whether the blue I see is the same blue you see — only that we have learned to agree on a word.

Language does not transmit experience.

It gestures toward it.

It sketches reality, but it does not hold it.

The Half-Truth Problem

Every word is a partial truth.

A mountain looks different from the valley than it does from the ridge above it. The mountain has not changed — only the vantage point.

So too with ideas.

Meaning is always filtered through experience, memory, identity, culture, belief, expectation — to name only a few. Language reflects this filtering. It cannot do otherwise.

This is why two people can hear the same sentence and

walk away with different understandings.

It is why sacred texts evolve in meaning across centuries.

Why philosophy remains endlessly debated.

Why the same poem can comfort one person and unsettle another.

Words are vessels.

Interpretation is what fills them.

Why Metaphor Matters

Literal language cannot reach the deeper layers of reality.

We rely on metaphor because it allows us to speak about things that resist direct description: consciousness, time, meaning, the unseen forces shaping experience, the patterns beneath what we observe.

Metaphors do not pretend to be the thing itself.

They offer a doorway into its character.

They allow us to say more than literal language would otherwise permit.

When I write of trees, rivers, branches, or threads, I am not suggesting that the universe is literally composed of these forms, nor bound by the limits we associate with their definitions. I am pointing instead to patterns — recurring shapes of behavior that echo across scales.

This is the Hermetic Principle of Correspondence:

As above, so below.

As within, so without.

I value this principle for the permission it grants. Pay close attention to what you can observe, and allow its reflection to resonate into what you cannot yet see — upward or inward, outward or beyond.

Nature is generous with its hints.

We see repeating patterns everywhere — documented in mathematics, physics, and the living geometry of form. This is no longer a fringe observation.

Metaphor becomes a decoder for what cannot yet be spoken directly.

Language as a Tool — and a Trap

We use language to describe our inner lives, explain beliefs, carry wisdom across time, shape identity, and build societies.

But we also use language to limit, categorize, oversimplify, confine the self, trap others in definitions, and enforce boundaries that no longer serve us.

A word can liberate.

A word can imprison.

"I am" can open infinite possibility.

"I am this or that" can quietly close it.

Definitions help us orient.

But they also draw borders where none truly exist.

The moment we name something, we reduce it.

The moment we define ourselves, we risk mistaking the definition for the whole.

Why This Work Must Use Language Carefully

The ideas ahead — time as a fractal, the present moment as a junction, the role of the Weaver, the threads of experience, the collapse of possibility — cannot be expressed without simplification. There are no words that do not flatten some aspect of their nature.

So this work will speak in images.

Time grows like a tree.

Reality unfolds like a tapestry.

Meaning is woven thread by thread.

Consciousness participates as a Weaver.

Experience arrives as vibration.

These are not claims about physical structure.

They are reflections of patterns that repeat across scale and experience.

To a strictly literal thinker, this may feel imprecise.

To a perceptive thinker, this is how truth often reveals itself — through echo, correspondence, and analogy.

We are approaching terrain where metaphor is not decoration, but necessity.

Interpretation Belongs to You

Your interpretation will always matter more than my intention.

No matter what I offer here, your interpretation completes the meaning.

I can outline an idea, but you fill it with lived experience.

I can describe a thread, but you must feel its texture.

I can point toward a pattern, but you must recognize it in your own life, and in your own time.

Language is shared.

Meaning is personal.

If something here resonates, follow that thread.

If something challenges you, sit with it.

If something feels unfamiliar, turn it in your mind like a

stone in your hand until its shape becomes clear.

Interpretation is not passive.

It is your first act of weaving.

And in truth, this entire work is an invitation to do just that — to weave with time, experience, and perspective.

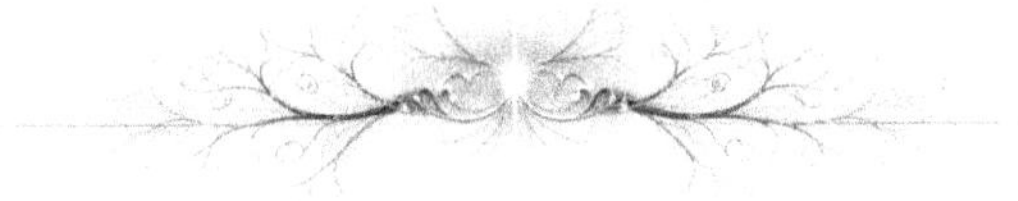

Now that we have acknowledged both the limits and power of language, we can begin to loosen the definitions you were taught about time.

Because to see time clearly, you must first let go of the idea that it moves in a straight line.

When we look at nature, we do not find straight lines.

Why would time be the exception?

Time behaves like something alive — branching, growing, responding, repeating patterns across scale.

Let this idea rest for now.

We will return to it in Part II, and begin to look more closely at what it reveals.

Chapter Three

The Human Toolkit

Human beings do not encounter the world empty-handed.

We arrive with a set of perceptual tools — ancient, subtle, and often unexamined — that shape how reality appears to us long before we learn the words to describe it.

Most people use these tools unconsciously, the way we breathe without thinking or walk without noticing the rhythm of our steps.

Before we can explore time, consciousness, or the weaving of experience, we must understand the instruments with which we perceive reality.

Because we cannot explore life with tools we do not recognize.

And we cannot reshape our understanding of reality while

holding the same assumptions about how we come to know anything at all.

This chapter is about those tools — the ones we inherit simply by being human, and the ones we often misuse without realizing it.

Observation

Before we can question, before we can explain, before we can construct meaning —we must first notice.

Observation is not an action we perform.

It is a condition of being alive.

The body observes continuously.

The senses gather data.

Patterns begin forming before thought has a chance to intervene.

Only afterward do curiosity, emotion, intuition, logic, and language engage.

Observation supplies the threads.

Without observation, nothing enters experience.

There is nothing to interpret, nothing to respond to, nothing to weave.

Later chapters will explore how observation shapes moments, collapses possibility, and builds the structure of time itself. For now, it is enough to recognize this:

Observation is the foundation upon which all understanding rests.

Please note: throughout this perspective, the words awareness and observation will appear closely related, and they are. They describe different aspects of the same living process.

Awareness refers to the range within which experience can be noticed — the openness of the field itself. Observation refers to the act of engagement within that field — the moment where contact occurs and experience takes shape.

Awareness shapes what can be seen. Observation shapes what becomes actual.

Emotion

Before we learned to speak, before we learned to reason, we felt.

Emotion is one of the oldest tools in human experience — older than language, older than thought, older even than the concept of "self." It is an original compass of consciousness.

Emotion guided early humans toward safety and connection, nourishment and belonging, long before explanation existed.

Emotion is not the opposite of reason.

It is the foundation upon which reason stands.

The mind interprets the world.

Emotion responds to it.

Fear sharpens attention.

Joy opens awareness.

Sadness softens the boundaries of the self.

Anger demands change.

Wonder expands possibility.

Every emotion is information — a message delivered in the language of sensation.

Because emotion speaks beneath words, we often misunderstand it. We treat it as a problem to solve rather than a signal to understand. Yet nearly every meaningful human decision — who we love, what we pursue, what we avoid, what we defend — is carried by emotional current.

Emotion is not weakness.

Emotion is guidance.

To explore time and consciousness, emotion must be recognized not as disruption, but as perception.

When we feel, we are already participating in the weave.

Intuition

If emotion is the body's language, intuition is the mind's quiet knowing — understanding that arrives before explanation.

Intuition is older than logic and faster than reason.

It does not shout.

It whispers.

It is the sense that something is right — or not — even when evidence has not yet formed.

Intuition is not guesswork.

It is pattern recognition operating beneath conscious awareness.

It draws from memory, emotion, experience, biology, and countless subtle cues the conscious mind never fully registers. It is the subconscious processing of an entire lived tapestry, distilled into a single moment of clarity.

Every breakthrough — scientific, artistic, philosophical — began as intuition.

Logic followed afterward.

Intuition senses the paths still forming.

Reason traces the paths already laid.

To trust intuition is not to abandon reason.

It is to engage a wider spectrum of perception.

The living time perspective emerged from intuition — whispers that grew louder until they demanded articulation.

Intuition is how the mind listens when the world has not yet spoken.

Pattern Recognition

Of all the human tools, pattern recognition may be the most fundamental.

Before mathematics, before symbols, before theory, humans noticed patterns:

- the sun's movement,
- the seasons' turn,
- the cycles of life and death.

Pattern recognition is how survival became understanding.

Science seeks patterns to explain and test reality.

Philosophy traces patterns in experience.

Art reveals patterns in form and meaning.

Human consciousness is a pattern-detecting instrument.

But pattern recognition is not purely analytical — it is

creative.

What we notice shapes what we believe.

What we believe shapes what we notice next.

This reciprocal dance fuels insight — and illusion.

Used consciously, pattern recognition reveals structure.

Used unconsciously, it can impose meaning where none exists.

Discernment is what keeps the tool aligned.

Later, when we explore time as a living, branching structure, pattern recognition will be essential. To see time clearly, we must learn to see beneath it.

Meaning-Making

Perhaps the most defining human trait is the compulsion to create meaning.

We do not merely experience life — we interpret it.

Meaning-making is not passive.

It is an act of creation.

Meaning is not simply found.

Meaning is woven.

Some follow this process unconsciously. Others feel compelled to pull at threads, question assumptions, and sit with uncertainty until understanding forms.

For me, meaning-making has never been optional.

Logic became a lantern in uncertainty — a way to navigate chaos without denying mystery. Meaning is crafted from experience, memory, emotion, and observation.

Because meaning is woven, and it can be rewoven.

This prepares us for what comes next.

The Arts

Before there was writing, before structured language, before philosophy itself, there was art.

Long before humans learned to name the world, we learned to feel it.

Art was the first bridge between inner and outer experience: the drumbeat echoing a heartbeat, the handprint on stone declaring *I was here*, the dance mirroring wind and flame, the carved figure carrying a story beyond a single lifetime.

The arts are humanity's oldest form of communication: music, movement, story, symbol, image.

Art does not describe emotion; it summons it.

It does not explain experience; it evokes it.

A song reaches into us and stirs something we cannot name — a recognition, a longing, a truth we forgot we carried.

A painting holds us still until we recognize ourselves in color, tension, or silence.

A story reshapes how we see the world — not by instruction, but by invitation.

The arts reveal a truth essential to this orientation:

Anything touched by consciousness becomes a thread another consciousness can weave with.

When a conscious being engages or creates, something of that encounter remains — a fractal imprint of emotion, intention, attention, or meaning — available for another consciousness to meet from its own position in time.

In other words, this exchange is not one-directional.

The artist expresses.

The observer receives.

A resonance forms.

And in that resonance, something transfers — a feeling, a question, a memory, a possibility.

The artwork becomes part of the observer's inner world.

The observer becomes part of the artwork's ongoing life.

Art is empathy made tangible.

It is the echo of another mind felt within our own.

This is why music lifts sorrow without words, why images outlive their creators, why myth endures long after cultures fade.

The arts are the earliest proof that consciousness is not confined to the mind.

It extends outward.

It imprints itself on form, symbol, gesture, and vibration.

In this way, art behaves like time itself: layered, resonant, alive, and continuously unfolding in meaning.

Art is the first loom.

And through it, we learn the earliest truth of weaving:

We are not alone in our inner worlds.

We are constantly weaving one another.

Language

Language is not the first tool we use — but it is the first distinctly human tool we learn to examine, refine, and transmit consciously.

It begins as sound: a cry, a laugh, a word spoken long before it is understood. From these simple vibrations, we build entire worlds.

Language does more than communicate; it constructs the framework of our thoughts.

We think in language.

We reason through language.

We understand ourselves largely through the stories we tell about who we are.

But here is the paradox:

Language expands our world, and at the same time, it limits the shape that world can take.

Every word is a boundary.

Every definition is a reduction.

Every sentence is a simplified model of an experience far richer than the symbols used to describe it.

Language transforms the infinite into the understandable — and in doing so, it sometimes hides the infinite from view.

Yet without language, we would be prisoners of our own minds.

Language is how we pass knowledge forward, how we share experience across time, how we bridge the space between two agents of consciousness.

Language is not reality.

It is the architecture within which reality becomes discussable.

Language is both a gift and a responsibility.

It is the doorway — not the destination.

Writing

If language shapes our inner world, writing anchors that world in time.

Writing is memory made visible.

It is the act of reaching into the fleeting stream of thought and pulling something solid back to shore.

A spoken word disappears as soon as breath leaves the body.

A written word can travel centuries without losing its shape.

This is writing's power — and its danger.

Writing preserves wisdom, but it also preserves misunderstanding.

It captures insight, but freezes it in the form it held at that moment.

A written idea is not a fixed truth.

It is a moment in consciousness, captured before it had the chance to grow.

And yet, writing remains one of humanity's greatest gifts.

It allows a child to learn from a teacher long gone.

It preserves stories that would otherwise vanish.

It enables dialogue across time.

This book exists because of writing.

Because ideas can only be woven together if they are placed into a form that can meet you in your own moment.

Writing is the loom upon which abstract thought takes physical form.

A word is a thread.

A paragraph is a strand.

A book is a tapestry.

Writing is not the end of understanding.

It is the beginning of dialogue.

And the moment you engage with these words, you join the weaving yourself.

This chapter has been about recognizing the tools.

The next will explore the force that influences how those tools shape lived experience.

Because before we can understand time, we must understand what determines which threads appear, which fade, and which shape the next moment of experience.

Chapter Four

What These Tools Reveal

Throughout human history, meaningful change has never come from tools alone, but from how they are used.

Observation, intuition, pattern recognition, language, art, and meaning-making have accompanied human experience across eras and cultures.

What shifts over time is not only the questions we ask with these tools, but the depth of awareness, refinement of use, and capacity of consciousness through which they are engaged.

When used with care, these tools expand understanding.

When used rigidly, they narrow it.

This chapter is not about belief.

It is about what has been revealed—again and again—when human beings learn to observe more closely and question more honestly.

Observation and the Scientific Expansion of Reality

Science begins not with answers, but with attention.

Every major scientific shift began when someone noticed that reality was behaving differently than expected. The motion of planets. The fall of an apple. The behavior of light. The structure of cells. The firing of neurons.

Observation gathered the data.

Curiosity asked the question.

Pattern recognition revealed coherence.

Language and mathematics attempted description.

At the smallest scales of reality, however, observation revealed something unexpected.

In quantum physics, matter does not behave as solid, independent objects moving cleanly through space. Instead, it behaves as probability—as potential—as fields of possibility that only resolve through interaction.

Experiments such as the double-slit experiment revealed that particles behave as fields of possibility, producing wave-like interference patterns. When a measuring interaction occurs, that field resolves into a single observed outcome.

Physics does not claim that human awareness creates reality. That is not what the data supports.

But it does show something equally important:

Interaction matters.

Measurement changes outcomes.

Observation is not irrelevant.

What these findings quietly suggest is not that reality is imagined into existence, but that participation plays a role in how potential resolves into experience. Observation does not invent the world—it participates in how possibility becomes actuality.

This marks a profound shift from the purely mechanical worldview that once dominated scientific thought. Reality is not merely there to be looked at. It responds when relationship is formed.

Ancient Insight and Modern Discovery

Long before instruments could measure particles or fields, ancient traditions relied on observation of a different kind. They watched nature closely—not to dominate it, but to understand its patterns.

They observed cycles: day and night, birth and death, growth and decay, expansion and return.

They noticed rhythm and repetition. They saw the same

structures appearing at different scales: in the heavens and the human body, in seasons and emotions, in sound, movement, and form.

From this, many cultures arrived at a shared insight: the many arise from the one.

In Hermetic philosophy, this appears as the Principle of Correspondence—as above, so below; as within, so without—the recognition that similar patterns repeat across scales of reality.

In Taoist thought, it appears as the Tao—the unnamable source from which all forms arise and to which they return.

In Vedic traditions, it appears as Brahman—the unified reality beneath appearances, with individual forms understood as temporary expressions of a deeper whole.

In ancient Greek philosophy, thinkers such as Parmenides and later the Stoics spoke of an underlying substance or logos that structured the cosmos.

These traditions did not rely on equations. Meaning was expressed through metaphor, symbol, geometry, myth, and lived experience. They were not attempting to predict particle behavior. They were attempting to understand relationship, unity, and process.

They were not unscientific.

They were pre-instrumental.

They used the tools available to them—observation, intuition, pattern recognition, language, art, and meaning-making—to articulate truths about balance, emergence, and interconnectedness.

Modern science approaches the same mystery from a different direction, shaped by different tools and constraints.

It does not speak of Tao or Brahman. It speaks of fields, probabilities, and indistinguishable particles. But it reveals something strikingly similar: that at the most fundamental level, reality is not composed of separate, independent objects, but of unified systems whose behavior becomes distinct only through interaction.

Science reveals how reality behaves.

Ancient traditions explored what that behavior might mean.

They are not competing narratives.

They are complementary lenses.

When either hardens into dogma, understanding collapses.

When both are held with humility, perspective expands.

The Danger of Rigid Frameworks

At various points in history, both science and religion have hardened into institutions that defend conclusions instead of curiosity.

When observation is filtered through ideology, data is ignored.

When meaning is forced into doctrine, experience is dismissed.

This is not a failure of tools.

It is a failure of use.

The same tools that expand understanding can narrow it when certainty replaces inquiry.

Why This Matters Here

This perspective does not ask for acceptance of a conclusion.

It asks for recognition of a pattern.

Across cultures, disciplines, and centuries, when human beings used their tools honestly—without clinging to rigid identity, without forcing premature answers—they discovered that reality is relational, participatory, layered, and far less static than once believed.

This understanding is not mystical.

It is not anti-scientific.

It is not new.

It is simply what becomes visible when observation is allowed to remain open.

What follows in these pages does not emerge from speculation alone, but from standing at the intersection of these long-running human inquiries. The tools have already shown us that reality is not as simple as we were once taught.

What remains is to understand the moment where these tools converge—the point at which observation, meaning, and experience meet, and the next moment takes shape.

Chapter Five

Culture, Society, and the Machinery of Distraction

Culture and society are not accidents.

They are expressions of human nature.

They arise from our need to belong, to cooperate, to share meaning, and to carry knowledge forward through time. They give us language, structure, continuity, and a sense of place within something larger than ourselves.

So this chapter is not a rejection of culture or society.

It is an invitation to see them more clearly.

Because everything that shapes us also directs us.

And everything that directs us influences how we experience ourselves, our time, and our world.

If the previous chapter stood at the edge of two ways of understanding reality—scientific and ancient—then this chapter steps closer to something more immediate and lived: the environment most of us inhabit every day.

Not nature.

Not the laboratory.

But the shared human current that surrounds us from birth.

To move into Part II with integrity, we need one final kind of preparation: a clear look at the forces that shape attention.

Culture as a Lens

Culture does not only shape how we live.

It shapes how we remember.

What we call history is not the past itself, but a cultural record of it—a curated thread pulled from countless lived experiences and arranged into something that can be followed, taught, and passed on.

We even name it in a way that reveals our bias: the timeline.

A single line. Ordered. Sequential. Cleanly divided into years, eras, ages, and turning points.

This structure is useful. It provides shared reference. It allows continuity between generations separated by time. Without it, collective learning would fracture.

But it is not the whole truth.

Culture determines which events are placed upon that line—and which are left out. What is preserved, emphasized, simplified, or erased depends not only on what happened, but on who held influence, who told the story, and what meaning a society needed at the time.

Entire civilizations have risen and fallen with little trace in the dominant record. Others are reduced to footnotes. Some voices are amplified; others are silenced. Complex realities are compressed into dates and names that fit neatly into textbooks.

This is not deception by design.

It is the consequence of limitation.

A culture can only preserve so much. It selects what aligns with its values, identity, and sense of progress. What does not fit the narrative often fades—not because it was unimportant, but because it was inconvenient, misunderstood, difficult to integrate, or...

Culture does not merely record time.

It edits it.

And that edit quietly shapes how we imagine time itself. When we inherit a singular, linear narrative of the past, we begin to picture time as linear as well—a straight path behind us, a straight path ahead.

Language reinforces this habit.

We speak of moving forward, falling behind, looking back, being ahead of our time. These phrases are useful—but they are metaphors we have forgotten are metaphors.

Recognizing this does not invalidate history.

It deepens it.

It allows recorded timelines to remain what they were meant to be: tools for orientation, not absolute representations of reality.

And it prepares a quieter, more important question:

If culture shapes how time is recorded, what else might it be shaping about how time is experienced?

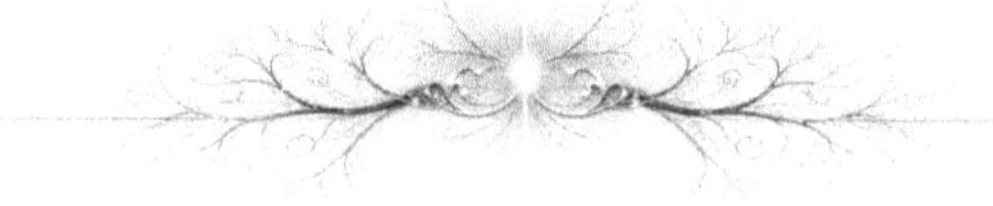

This is how culture presents time: organized, shared, and flattened into continuity.

The Living Time Perspective begins where this presentation reaches its limit — not in the record of what happened, but in the moment where experience occurs.

It acknowledges the complexity of the structure and turns toward what cannot be hidden, edited, or rearranged: the personal relationship we hold with time and the contribution to the collective experience.

It begins not with history as it is told, but with the present moment as it is lived — where time takes shape through direct engagement rather than inherited narrative.

The Direction of Attention

Culture does not grow at random.

Like anything alive, it grows where nourishment is given.

Ideas strengthen when they are repeated.

Beliefs harden when they are shared.

Movements expand when attention flows toward them.

You can observe this everywhere.

A phrase, a song, a headline, a story—once it captures attention, it spreads. What felt unfamiliar becomes normal. What was questioned becomes assumed. Not always because it is true, but because it is encountered repeatedly.

Repetition creates familiarity.

Familiarity creates comfort.

Comfort creates acceptance.

Throughout history, cultural leaders—artists, thinkers,

storytellers, scientists, spiritual teachers—have served as focal points for collective attention. They did not simply reflect culture; they helped direct it. They gave language to experiences others had not yet been able to articulate.

This is not manipulation by default.

It is leadership.

But direction always implies exclusion. Not everything can be illuminated at once. Attention is finite. Where it gathers, something grows. Where it is absent, something withers.

In modern life, attention is guided at a scale unprecedented in human history. Platforms, algorithms, institutions, and incentives shape what enters awareness—not only through what is shown, but through what is repeated, prioritized, and framed as urgent.

This does not require malice.

It follows from incentive.

When attention becomes currency, those who hold it gain influence over what grows next.

And because attention shapes perception, it also shapes experience.

What we notice becomes what we think about.

What we think about becomes what we discuss.

What we discuss becomes what we reinforce—in ourselves

and in others.

This is how shared realities form.

There is no accusation here.

Only an invitation to observe.

Because the moment we recognize that attention participates in growth, we regain something essential: *choice.*

Not total control—but orientation.

Productivity and the Compression of Time

Time is one of the most powerful organizing forces of modern life.

Schedules, deadlines, calendars, clocks—these structures allow coordination on a massive scale. They enable cooperation, innovation, and continuity. Without them, much of what we depend on would collapse.

Time, in this sense, is not the enemy.

It is a tool.

But tools shape perception.

Within productivity culture, time gradually shifts in character. It stops being something we live and becomes something we manage.

Time becomes scarce.

Time becomes something to use, save, spend, or lose.

Time becomes external—a resource rather than a rhythm.

Moments are measured not by depth or meaning, but by output. The present is valued primarily for what it produces next. Rest becomes recovery. Stillness becomes inefficiency. Waiting becomes waste.

This compression changes how time feels.

Days blur together.

Weeks accelerate.

Years seem to vanish faster than they arrived.

Not because time itself has changed — but because our relationship to it has.

From that viewpoint, time is experienced as one-dimensional: forward, relentless, demanding. We speak of being behind, ahead, on track, running out of time.

And yet, even within this narrow view, contradictions remain.

We feel cycles.

We honor seasons.

We sense ebb and return.

We say history repeats itself.

These are quiet acknowledgments that time may not be as

simple as a straight line.

But productivity culture rarely lingers there. The schedule marches forward. The body signals rhythm. The calendar demands consistency.

The result is not failure.

It is friction.

A friction between how time is lived and how time is measured.

This is not a call to abandon structure.

It is an invitation to notice the cost of flattening time into a single dimension.

Because when time is treated only as a resource, presence thins.

When rhythm is ignored, meaning weakens.

When every moment is oriented toward the next, the present loses depth.

And still—something in us keeps whispering that there is more.

Fear, Media, and the Pull of Urgency

Fear is one of the most efficient ways to command attention.

It sharpens focus.

It narrows perception.

It pulls awareness into the immediate moment and holds it there.

This is not a flaw in human nature.

It is a survival mechanism.

Fear evolved to help organisms respond to real, present danger. It mobilizes energy, prioritizes action, and reduces hesitation when speed matters. But fear was never designed to remain active beyond the moment of necessity.

What has changed is not the emotion itself, but how far and how long it can now be carried.

Human beings possess a unique ability: we can project emotion beyond the present moment. We imagine futures, rehearse outcomes, and construct narratives about what might happen. This capacity is one of our greatest strengths—but it also makes us vulnerable.

Fear can now be projected forward through time.

Into imagined tomorrows.

Into collective stories.

Into possibilities that may never arrive.

When fear is repeatedly projected, it no longer signals immediate danger—it becomes atmosphere.

In modern life, fear often arrives indirectly—through

screens, alerts, headlines, images, and repetition. The nervous system responds as if the threat were present and personal, even when it is distant, abstract, unresolved, or uncertain.

Urgency becomes ambient.

This sustained alertness has predictable effects.

Attention contracts.

Reflection weakens.

Emotional regulation becomes more difficult.

In this state, the mind becomes more suggestible—not because it is weak, but because it is overloaded. It naturally follows threads that appear to promise safety, certainty, or relief.

What is repeated feels important.

What is framed as urgent feels unavoidable.

What is emotionally charged feels meaningful.

This does not require conspiracy or intent.

Again, it follows from incentive.

In systems where attention carries value, capturing and holding it becomes advantageous. Calm engagement can be profitable. Outrage can be profitable. Fear can be profitable. Distraction can be profitable. None of this requires malice—only structure.

This work does not ask you to reject media, withdraw from society, or assign blame. It asks for something quieter—and more difficult:

Notice the relationship between what you are shown, how you feel in response, and what you are encouraged to do next.

Fear shortens time.

Urgency flattens perspective.

Awareness does not eliminate these forces—but it loosens their grip.

And when that grip loosens, something else becomes possible:

A slower kind of seeing.

A wider field of attention.

A present moment that is no longer entirely shaped by what demands you react.

Identity and the Conveyor Belt

In a complex world, identity offers stability.

It gives language to describe ourselves, roles to inhabit, and belonging within the larger structure of society. Identity helps us orient.

These identities are not false.

They are functional.

But identity becomes limiting when it hardens.

Modern culture often presents identity as something to be selected, declared, defended, and maintained—as if the self were a finished product rather than a living process.

This hardening rarely happens through force.

It happens through repetition.

Systems reward coherence. Platforms reinforce labels. Belonging is often granted through alignment rather than exploration.

Identity becomes a conveyor belt.

Once stepped onto, it carries us forward along a narrow track—reinforcing certain behaviors, beliefs, and futures while making others less visible.

This shapes how time is experienced.

When identity is rigid, the future feels predetermined. The past becomes something to justify. Change feels dangerous—not because it is impossible, but because it threatens coherence.

And yet, beneath every label, something remains fluid.

Identity is not essence.

It is position.

The problem is not that we adopt identities.

The problem is forgetting that we can leave them.

Awareness restores movement.

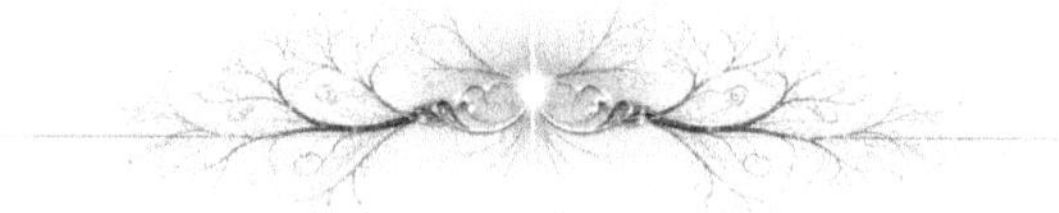

Culture, productivity, fear, attention, identity—these are not enemies of understanding. They are the environment in which understanding must occur.

They shape us because they must.

They influence us because they are powerful.

But influence is not the same as fate.

Part I of this book has not been about rejecting the world as it is. It has been about learning to see it more clearly—to recognize the forces already at work, and to restore awareness where it has quietly narrowed.

Before stepping into the deeper nature of time, it was necessary to pause here.

Not to escape these structures.

But to stand within them more consciously.

Because the next step will ask you to look at time itself—not as a line we move along, but as a living structure that grows through experience.

And to approach that honestly, one final recognition is needed:

Attention is not just something we spend.

It is something we place.

The present is where that placement occurs.

And where it is placed, something becomes real.

PART II — THE NATURE OF TIME

A LINE IS ONE-DIMENSIONAL.

It has length, but no depth. No width. No interior.

It stretches in a single direction—or two opposing directions—from one point to another.

This is how many of us were taught to think about time.

We open history books and see events labeled along an organized line.

Our tools mark everything ahead of us in hours, days, months, and years.

Past behind us.

Future ahead.

And the present slipping endlessly forward, as if time is something simply happening to us.

It is a useful model. It allows coordination, measurement, and prediction.

But usefulness does not guarantee completeness. It is another half-truth.

If time were truly one-dimensional, it would behave like a line.

And yet we would be making time the only thing in nature we insist on viewing that way.

Rivers do not travel directly to the sea.

Wind curves, spirals, and returns.

Light bends, reflects, refracts, and changes direction.

Even planets move in arcs rather than lines.

In the living world, straight lines are the exception. Patterns and movement are the rules.

Cycles, curves, feedback, growth.

If almost nothing else we observe behaves like a line, why would time?

Even our own experience contradicts it.

We all experience time differently.

Memory does not stay behind us.

Anticipation reaches forward.

Patterns return.

Moments echo.

"History repeats itself."

"Time flies when you're having fun."

"That day would never end."

And the older we get, the faster time seems to go.

We have practical explanations for these experiences, and this perspective does not deny them.

The clock ticks with steady precision, and in many important ways it does so equally for all of us.

The Living Time Perspective does not attempt to replace what we already know.

It offers another way of seeing the same half-truth—it shows a more personal relationship with time, one that may quietly alter your relationship with life itself.

If time is not one-dimensional, then it must be something more.

How many dimensions it has, I cannot say.

But I will suggest that its lived structure has at least three.

I say this not as certainty, but as an acknowledgment of complexity.

Any incompleteness or apparent contradiction you encounter ahead may not be a mistake to correct, but a signal—of the limits of language, and of the human mind trying to describe something larger than itself.

This perspective is imperfect because it is human.

That is not a flaw. It is the condition that makes further exploration necessary.

What follows is not an argument to be proven, but a perspective to inhabit— a way of looking that may reveal relationships you have already felt, but never fully examined.

In my experience, time behaves less like a line and more like something alive.

It grows.

Like lightning branching across a sky.

Like a plant reaching toward the sun.

Like streams merging into a river.

You are free to choose your own metaphors.

I am drawn to the image of a growing tree—not because it is precise, but because it is familiar, layered, and honest in its complexity.

The tree of life. The flower of life.

These symbols have long held weight in my own journey, and perhaps that is why this form feels natural here.

We already sense the connection in quieter ways: the family tree—generations branching, intersecting, and giving rise to what follows.

And yet this metaphor has a limitation.

We do not create living trees.

We observe them.

So when this lens turns toward our personal relationship with time—our interaction with the present moment—I often shift to a different image:

A tapestry.

Threads and fibers woven into a fabric we can touch, alter, and influence.

Not because it is more accurate, but because it is more relatable.

Both metaphors point toward the same underlying pattern.

Neither should be taken literally. They are tools for seeing the unseeable—nothing more.

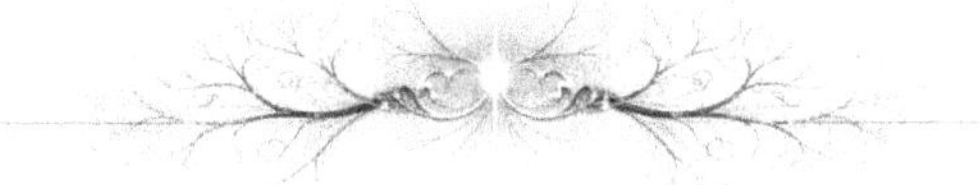

If time is alive, then it has structure.

If it grows, then it has anatomy.

And if it has anatomy, then it can be studied—not with instruments, but with attention.

That is where this part of the work begins to take us next.

In the chapters ahead, we will explore time the way we might explore any living system we wish to understand: by observing its patterns, its growth, its intersections, and its cycles— the way the unseen gives rise to the seen, the way motion becomes rhythm, the way repetition becomes meaning.

I offer no proof. Only perspective.

What I share here resonates as true to my own experience—shaped by observation, reflection, and the slow weaving of understanding over my time.

For you, these ideas may land differently.

At best, they will remain half-truths—shaped by your own history, your own vantage point, your own moment of encounter, your own time.

That is not a flaw.

It is the point.

If any of this feels unfamiliar, resist the urge to dismiss it too quickly.

Sit with it. Let it unfold slowly.

Perspective changes with patience.

What follows will sometimes borrow language from science, philosophy, and lived experience without fully belonging to any one of them. This is intentional.

The Living Time Perspective is not an attempt to explain reality in absolute terms, but to explore how it is encountered. Where certainty would flatten the inquiry, ambiguity has been allowed to remain.

We begin now — not by abandoning what we know, but by loosening our grip on it, just enough to see what might be growing all around us.

Chapter Six

All Living Things Start Somewhere

Let us begin by stepping away from the simplicity of a line.

Living things do not grow in straight paths. They grow through branching, adaptation, response, and relationship. They change direction when conditions change. They carry memory within their structure. And they begin — or at least emerge — from something that resembles a beginning.

If time is alive, it should be no different.

The textbooks I grew up with pointed to something called the Big Bang as the beginning of the universe, and of time as we understand it. But this is not the only way human beings have tried to name that first moment.

Across cultures and traditions, the same origin has been described in different languages. Some speak of a word spoken into the void. Others of a breath moving across the waters. Still others of a vibration arising within formlessness, or a divine thought awakening itself into expression. Hermetic teaching names this origin Mentalism — the recognition that all things begin as potential before they appear as form.

Each of these perspectives holds a fragment of truth. None of them hold the whole.

So walk with me for a moment into another way of seeing — not a replacement for what came before, but another incomplete truth offered alongside the rest.

All living things begin from a point of origin.

A seed splits open in darkness. Biology has observed the zinc spark that flashes when sperm meets egg — a brief ignition that signals the beginning of a complex unfolding. In a single moment, a process is set in motion that will grow in structure, differentiation, and relationship.

The universe — and time itself — may not be so different.

What we have come to call the Big Bang is often imagined as an explosion: matter hurled outward into emptiness. It is a powerful image, but also a misleading one. Explosions imply chaos, dissipation, and eventual slowing. Seen through that lens, the accelerating expansion of the universe becomes puzzling.

The confusion may lie not in the observation, but in the metaphor.

What if the beginning was not an explosion, but an ignition?

A spark — like the zinc flash of life — marking the moment time and matter began unfolding together.

Living systems do not expand because they are thrown outward. They expand because something within them is organizing itself. A seed does not burst into a tree. A fertilized egg does not explode into a body. They grow — guided by internal coherence and emergent instruction, not by external force alone.

Seen this way, the universe behaves less like debris from a blast and more like a living structure coming into form.

Perhaps this is why the universe does not expand at a constant rate. It does not slow as an explosion would. Perhaps, like a growing organism, it experiences periods of rapid change — driven by internal dynamics we do not yet fully understand.

As with any living system, growth brought complexity.

From the first moment, the universe and time grew together — expanding, differentiating, and organizing into increasing structure. Expansion allowed distinction. Distinction allows relationship. Relationship allowed sequence. And sequence made memory possible.

Direction emerged not because time was pointed, but because interactions accumulated.

As movement appeared, vibration followed. As vibration

stabilized, rhythm formed. Patterns began to repeat. Cycles arose.

At this stage, something subtle but essential occurred.

The first lasting distinction took hold.

In a perfectly symmetrical state, nothing stands out. No direction is preferred. No structure can persist. It is a game of pong, where the paddles never move and the ball travels the same path indefinitely. For form to arise, symmetry must give way — not through destruction, but through differentiation. A slight imbalance allows one possibility to resolve instead of another. Once that happens, relationship occurs and structure can form.

In religious language, this is described as light separating from darkness. In Hermetic terms, polarity appears. In physical terms, symmetry breaks — allowing distinct forms, behaviors, and relationships to emerge.

This is not a contradiction between languages. It is the same moment described from different scales, from different perspectives.

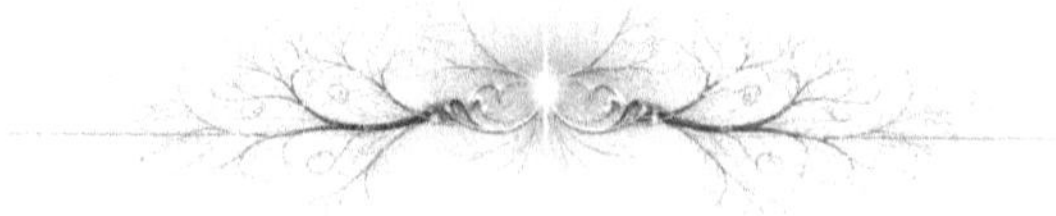

Time, like life, did not arrive fully formed.

It developed. It thickened. It gained texture as interactions layered upon one another. Each distinction made the next possible. Each relationship added depth. Each cycle carried memory forward.

What we experience now is not time as a static backdrop against which life unfolds, but time as a living process — one that has been growing ever since the first moment potential became expression.

Chapter Seven

The Shape Time Has Grown Into

Before we move inward, we need to look at the shape time has already grown into.

We have no way of seeing the full structure of time directly. No instrument allows us to step outside of it and observe it whole. But we do have something else: the tools we explored in Part I — observation, pattern recognition, and meaning-making.

When these tools are used together, they allow us to form reasonable images — not of what time is, but of how it behaves.

Throughout history, human beings have noticed that life follows patterns. Some repeat so consistently that they feel familiar even before we learn their names.

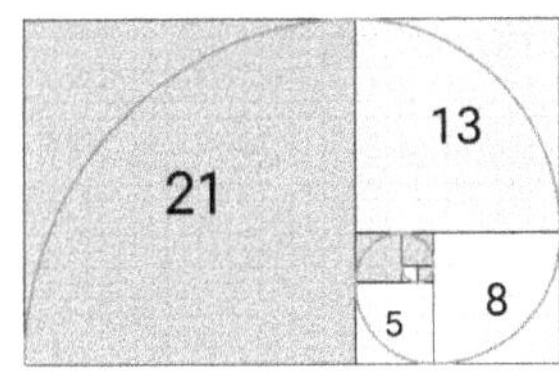

0, 1, 1, 2, 3, 5, 8, 13, 21...

Many will recognize this as the Fibonacci sequence — one of the most widely observed patterns in nature. It appears in the branching of trees, the spirals of shells, the arrangement of petals, and even the structure of galaxies.

At first glance, one might imagine that *time* follows a similar form: a graceful curve unfolding forward, orderly and predictable. This image is comforting. It preserves continuity and keeps time close to the idea of a line — merely bent rather than transformed.

But this, too, is only a partial view.

When we look more closely at the mathematics underlying living systems, far more complex structures appear.

Consider fractals.

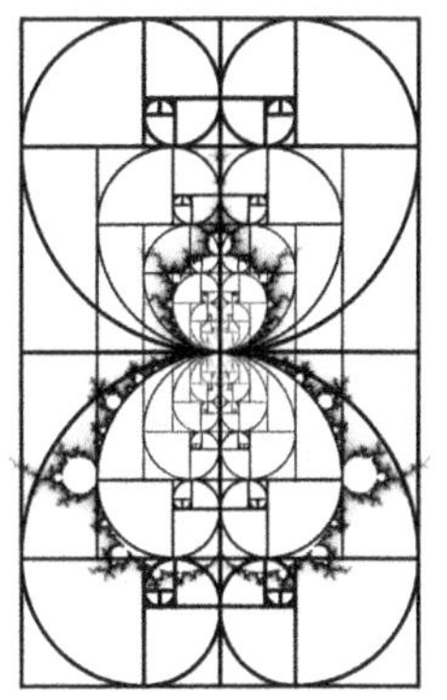

Image by Phil Bryan

Unlike simple curves, fractals reveal patterns that repeat across scales. A small portion resembles the whole — not perfectly, but unmistakably. The Mandelbrot set is one such structure, infinitely complex and endlessly revealing. One of its visual expressions, known as the Buddhabrot, carries a striking resemblance to a seated Buddha — a reminder that meaning often emerges not from intention, but from attentive observation.

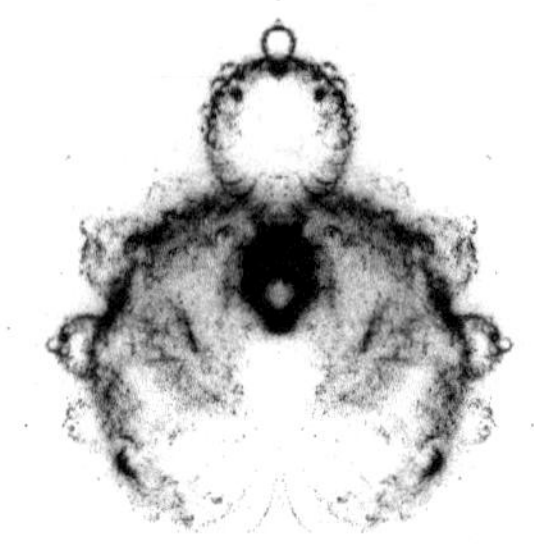

These patterns are not new. Variations of fractal geometry appear in sacred architecture, ancient symbols, ritual forms, and spiritual art across cultures and eras. Different civilizations, separated by time and geography, appear to have perceived the same underlying order — expressing it through the tools of meaning most available to them at the time: spatial design, symbol, rhythm, myth, and only gradually, articulated language.

Following that path too far would take us away from our purpose here. I pause only to acknowledge something important: those who came before us were not less perceptive. They were standing at different vantage points, with different tools of perception.

For the Living Time Perspective, we turn to a particular fractal form that appears again and again in living systems — one that resembles the branching of a tree.

A tree begins as a trunk. The trunk divides into large branches. Those branches divide again into smaller ones, and again into twigs. At every level, the same underlying logic of growth is present, adapted to scale and circumstance.

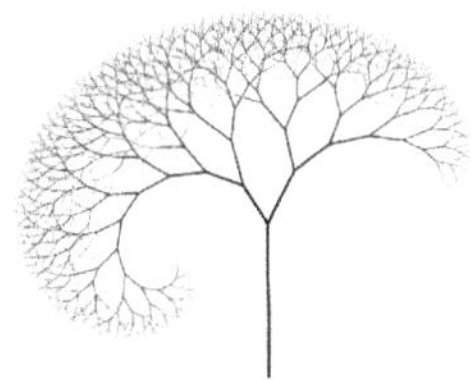

This structure is not accidental.

Fractal branching allows living systems to maximize connection, distribution, and resilience within finite space. Water, nutrients, energy, and information move efficiently through branching networks. Stress is distributed. Damage can be absorbed without total collapse.

Nature does not favor straight lines. It favors patterns that adapt.

If time is not a static backdrop but a living structure, it would be reasonable to expect it to exhibit similar characteristics.

Not repetition of events — but repetition of patterns.

At this point, a hesitation may arise.

You may wonder if I am suggesting that time branches? That it splits into different directions? That there is another time than the one we are experiencing.

Possibly.

But we do not need to explore that idea fully here.

The concept of branching time can feel speculative, especially when introduced outside formal mathematics or physics. That discomfort is reasonable. And it is worth noting that this idea does not arise solely from metaphor.

In quantum physics, there exists a framework known as the Many Worlds Interpretation. In simplified terms, it proposes that all possible outcomes of a quantum event continue to exist— not as discarded possibilities, but as distinct branches of reality in parallel to our own.

This idea is not introduced here as a conclusion, but as a familiar scientific echo of a structure we are observing.

Where the Living Time Perspective begins to differ is not in the idea of branching itself, but in the language we use to imagine it.

The word parallel is revealing.

Parallel lines imply separation without interaction — paths that move forward side by side, never touching, never influencing one another. This is a useful abstraction, but it is distinctly human.

Nature rarely behaves this way.

Rivers branch, but they also rejoin. Roots divide, but they intertwine. Ecosystems diverge and converge. Weather systems split, collapse, and recombine.

Growth in nature is not parallel. It is relational.

From this perspective, time does not unfold into isolated lines marching independently toward the future. It grows like a living system — branching, folding, merging, and sometimes looping back upon itself.

This distinction matters.

It allows memory, meaning, and influence to move through time not as sealed compartments, but as currents within a shared field. It allows continuity without requiring complete separation.

At the level of lived experience, this fluidity sometimes reveals itself in subtle ways.

One example is what has come to be known as the Mandela Effect — the experience of many people recalling events differently from what is currently recorded. Whether explained through psychology, culture, memory, or something not yet fully understood, it highlights an important observation:

Our experience of the past is not as fixed as our timelines suggest.

The Living Time Perspective does not claim that history rewrites itself or that memories slip between universes. It simply leaves room for the possibility that time, like memory, may be more fluid than a single, immutable line.

Again, this is not proof. Only perspective.

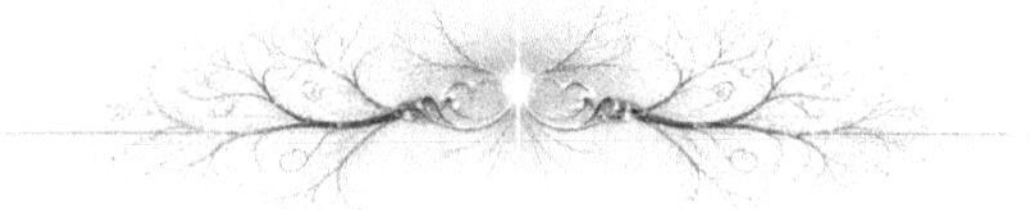

The images used here are necessarily simplified. They are two-dimensional representations of something that is not. Time is not hollow. Like any living system, what makes it function, is what happens inside — all the way down to the smallest scales we can observe, and beyond those we cannot.

And like any fractal, the pattern repeats at every level.

As we zoom inward, the vast branching of cosmic time begins to resolve into more intimate scales. One branch reflects time as experienced from Earth. Within that, branches of culture. Of language. Of shared history.

Zoom further, and we find families. Communities. Individuals. Thoughts. Dreams. Objects. Moments.

If you can experience it, it has a history. And if it has a history, it occupies its own place within time's structure.

This leads us to one of the central insights of the Living Time Perspective:

You are not generic. You are not interchangeable.

You occupy a singular position within time — shaped by a history no one else carries, meeting each moment from a vantage point that has never existed before and will never exist again.

You share threads with others — family, culture, place, era — but you never share them all. No one sees through your exact convergence of memory, feeling, instinct, and awareness.

Your experience is never fully shared. Never fully replicated.

And yet, it matters immensely.

Not in isolation, and not in dominance — but in contribution. Each moment you live, each choice you make, each meaning you allow to take root becomes part of a larger tapestry that could not exist without your thread woven exactly where it is.

You are not separate from the whole. You are one of the ways it happens.

And still, we are not meant to hold the entire picture at once.

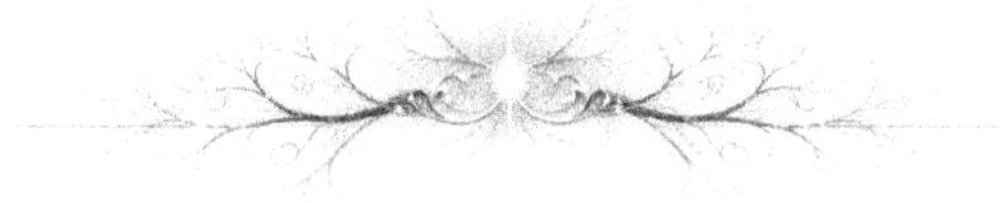

Perspective depends on distance. Meaning changes with scale.

What feels singular up close becomes complex and interwoven when viewed from farther away.

If we could see all of this at once, without shifting scale, it would not resemble a tidy tree. It would look tangled, layered, and alive.

Here, the tree metaphor begins to strain.

It serves us well at a distance, but lived experience is less rigid and more interwoven. For this reason, the metaphor shifts.

From tree to tapestry.

A tapestry allows us to speak about overlap, tension, texture, and pattern. It captures how moments are formed not only by growth, but by interaction — how meaning emerges from threads crossing in motion.

Each thread is spun from many fibers.

A diamond ring may be admired in the present, but it carries the history of carbon, pressure, labor, culture, and intention. It is a thread woven from many others.

All of these threads converge in the present moment. They create the structure of experience.

Which brings us to the next question:

What is it that makes this structure grow?

Chapter Eight

An Engine of Time

To understand how time grows, we must first understand how it is placed — how it becomes anchored to the living structure that exists before and beyond any single moment.

There is a simplified explanation I could offer about time, consciousness, and reality:

Everything exists as infinite probability until it is observed.

This statement points in a useful direction.

But on its own, it carries more weight than language can safely support.

Left unexplored, it invites misunderstanding — the impression that reality is imagined into existence, or that observation creates the world from nothing. That is not what this perspective claims, and it is not what science suggests either.

So before we go any further, we need to slow down.

To do that, we return to a tool introduced in Part I and revisited throughout this work:

Observation.

Observation as Participation, Not Spectatorship

A tree does not grow by chance alone.

It grows in response to conditions: light, water, soil, resistance, space.

The seed contains potential, but the shape that potential takes depends on what it encounters — and on how those encounters are converted into the energy required for growth.

In much the same way, the growth of time is shaped by interaction: by what is met, sustained, resisted, or ignored.

Within the Living Time Perspective, observation is not treated as passive witnessing.

It is treated as participation.

What is observed becomes part of the structure.

What is ignored weakens, thins, and fades.

What is repeated thickens.

What is resisted reshapes growth.

All living things survive by converting energy into their being. Where the energy flows, life flourishes.

From an individual perspective, this is visible in practices such as behavioral therapy. A familiar example is habit change. While the exact timeframe varies, the principle is consistent: when a habit no longer receives attention, reinforcement, or emotional energy, it weakens. When attention is redirected, energy flows into a new path. Over time, that path becomes easier to follow, while the old one fades from accessibility.

This process does not occur only at the personal level.

Shift the scale, and the same pattern appears in cultures, religions, nations, and social systems. What receives sustained observation and reinforcement continues to grow. What is gradually removed from attention — questioned, neglected, or no longer repeated — eventually loses structure and influence.

Awareness, observation, attention — however we name them — function like nutrients within th living system of time. They do not force growth, but they determine where growth remains viable.

From Possibility to Experience

Prior to the present moment, countless possibilities exist — conditioned by history, environment, momentum, and constraint.

Only a small fraction of those possibilities ever enter our experience.

From within this perspective, observation is the means by which possibility collapses into actuality and becomes the present experience.

To say that possibilities "collapse" is not to suggest a dramatic event, but a practical one: out of many potential interactions, one becomes observed, therefore actualized. In that collapse exists an immense amount of energy where actuality is welded into the existing structure of unfolding time.

The moment does not merely pass — it solidifies as the present moment.

It becomes part of structure.

It becomes memory.

It becomes the condition for what can happen next.

Energy and the Present Moment

At this point, it may be helpful to continue with what is already familiar.

If the Big Bang is an accurate description of the universe's beginning, it marks a moment of extraordinary energy — the ignition from which everything we can measure has unfolded. And if the law of conservation of energy holds — that energy is neither created nor destroyed — then the energy present in the universe now is not new. It is the same energy, redistributed, reorganized, and continuously expressed through interaction.

What becomes more speculative — and therefore must be handled carefully — is how we relate that to the present moment.

When possibility resolves into experience, something enormous occurs. Not necessarily in spectacle, but in organization. Every interaction involves energy: movement, exchange, transformation, pattern. The present moment is the site where those interactions actually happen — where potential becomes arranged into a particular outcome rather than remaining open as conditioned possibility.

From this perspective, the present moment can be understood as an echo of that original ignition — not in space, but in time. Not a repetition, but a continuation: the same conserved energy meeting fresh conditions, forming fresh structure, again and again.

So the present moment is not where energy originates.

It is where energy participates.

And if time is a living structure that grows through interaction, then the question becomes unavoidable: what influences where that energy engages?

The Living Time Perspective suggests that observation — awareness directed toward particular threads — plays a role in shaping that engagement. Not by inventing reality, but by participating in which potentials become lived experience, reinforced, and carried forward into the next moment of growth.

Why Some Threads Strengthen and Others Fade

Within this framework, observation does not create threads. It influences which threads are able to engage with the conditions of the present moment. Possibilities that remain unobserved do not become part of the lived unfolding of a given branch of time.

Threads that enter experience tend to strengthen, as if feeding on the energy of the present.

Threads that remain consistently unengaged tend to weaken without the *power of now.*

Over time, some become difficult to access — not necessarily erased, but too subtle to be engaged from all levels of conscious awareness.

All of this unfolds far beyond deliberate perception.

From the human vantage point, consciousness fills in continuity effortlessly. We experience a seamless flow, even though countless micro-interactions are occurring beneath awareness. You can see this in your own field of vision: clarity at the center, fading toward the periphery. Much of what you "see" is inferred, completed, or assumed.

Time behaves in a similar way.

When awareness is present in the moment, engagement becomes more precise. The available energy of the present is met directly rather than carried forward by momentum alone.

When awareness is absent — or cannot reach — patterns tend to repeat. The thickest branches carry the most accumulated structure. They require little attention to continue, because they have already been reinforced through repetition.

When awareness is present, growth becomes more responsive.

Awareness does not force change.

It alters viability.

Like water and nutrients in a living system, attention does not dictate form — it determines where growth remains possible.

This is not control.

It is relationship.

Human Awareness Within a Larger Field

Humans are not the only conscious participants in this process. Observation unfolds across countless forms of life, systems, and scales.

Human awareness, however, carries a particular intensity. Without requiring belief, it represents the most capable instrument of consciousness we have yet encountered.

Our capacity for reflection, imagination, memory, and sustained attention allows us to participate more deliberately in the ongoing structure of time.

Energy does not respond to force alone.

It responds to engagement.

Where attention is consistently placed, vitality gathers.

Where meaning is sustained, growth becomes possible.

This does not grant dominion over the present moment.

But it does confer responsibility within it.

You are not the sole weaver — but you are a significant one.

A Cautious Parallel with Physics

At this point, a familiar scientific echo may arise.

In quantum physics, experiments such as the double-slit experiment reveal something counterintuitive: at very small scales, systems do not behave like solid objects moving predictably through space. Instead, they behave as probability distributions—fields of potential outcomes that only resolve into specific results through interaction.

When no measurement is made, the system is described mathematically as existing in a range of possible states. When a measurement occurs—when the system is interacted with in a way that extracts information—those possibilities resolve into a definite outcome.

One interpretation of this behavior is known as the Copenhagen Interpretation. In simplified terms, it suggests that physical systems do not possess definite, measurable properties prior to measurement. This does not mean that reality is imagined into existence by human thought, nor that consciousness "creates" the physical world. It means that interaction plays a fundamental role in how potential becomes actual.

Physics stops there. It reports behavior, models outcomes, and resists assigning meaning beyond what can be measured.

The Living Time Perspective does not claim that human experience operates by the same physical mechanisms as quantum systems. It does not suggest that attention collapses wave functions, or that consciousness directly alters particles.

But the structural resemblance is difficult to ignore.

In both cases:

- Potential exists prior to interaction
- Interaction shapes which outcome becomes realized
- Observation participates in resolution, even if it does not invent what appears

This parallel is not offered as proof, but as orientation.

It suggests a pattern that appears across scales: that reality does not unfold independently of engagement, and that structure forms where possibility meets interaction.

From within the Living Time Perspective, time grows in the same way. Not because it is forced. Not because it is commanded. But because interaction selects, reinforces, and carries certain paths forward.

The present moment becomes the site of that engagement. Not the origin of possibility, but the place where possibility takes form.

An Invitation, Not a Conclusion

This chapter does not ask you to accept these ideas as fact.

It asks you to sit with them long enough to notice how they alter your experience of the present moment. It invites you to participate as an active observer in the unfolding of your experience, while pointing to a potential logical explanation of how it is formed.

If this helps you see what is already happening — just beneath the surface of now — then it has served its purpose.

What follows depends not on belief, but on whether this way of seeing allows you to recognize your own participation more clearly.

Because if time is alive, then every moment of attention matters — not as control, but as contribution.

And the present moment is where that contribution always occurs.

Chapter Nine

The Present Moment as a Junction

Up to this point, we have been looking at time from a distance.

We have stepped back far enough to see its shape — how it grows, how it branches, how it thickens into structure. We have spoken about beginnings, patterns, and the large-scale architecture of living time.

But no living thing can be understood only from afar.

A tree is not known by its silhouette alone.

A body is not understood by its outline.

A river is not revealed by its direction on a map.

Structure matters — but function lives inside.

To understand how time actually unfolds, we now have to move closer. Not inward in a metaphysical sense, but inward in scale — toward the smallest unit of time that is still alive with meaning.

The present moment.

In the previous chapter, we touched on a reflection that may have felt unsettling: that the present moment contains an immense amount of energy — perhaps comparable, in some sense, to the energy present at the universe's beginning, often described as the Big Bang.

I want to pause here and acknowledge a necessary half-truth in that statement.

I cannot know whether all of the energy from that first moment exists in the present, or whether some remains embedded within the structure of time already formed or the branching of time we will never experience. It is entirely possible that this, too, is a matter of perspective.

The statement is not meant to be precise.

It is meant to emphasize scale.

Whatever the exact accounting, the present moment carries extraordinary power — enough to continuously give rise to what comes next.

In this chapter, we will look more closely at what exists within the present moment — and how that moment functions.

Defining the Field of View

The present moment is still a broad field. To speak about it meaningfully, we must narrow our perspective.

First, we limit our reference point to Earth. From here we understand years, months, hours, seconds — measurements calibrated to Earth's movement through space.

Earth itself can be thought of as an observation point unfolding within the fractal of time, but that perspective is difficult to relate to directly. So we narrow again — to the scale of human experience.

I will not define the length of a present moment. That cannot be done cleanly from our vantage point.

Instead, imagine the present as unfolding across a near infinite number of frames per second — a rate far beyond what our senses can register. At this scale, countless interactions occur without ever entering human-conscious awareness.

This is the present moment we are trying to understand.

The Ingredients of a Moment

We have already identified three primary elements that meet within the present moment:

- Energy
- Conscious observation

- Threads

Energy and consciousness may feel familiar enough as concepts. We will explore consciousness in much greater detail in the next chapter.

But what is a thread?

A thread is anything a conscious being can engage with.

This includes physical objects with mass — but also non-tangible elements of creation: thoughts, emotions, memories, expectations, dreams, etc.

If consciousness can interact with it, it functions as a thread.

A thread holds a very broad meaning in the infancy of the Living Time Perspective. I expect this understanding and meaning to evolve through me, and through others who choose to work with it.

There are likely other elements involved in the formation of a moment, but these three are sufficient for our purposes here.

Within each present moment, a reaction occurs when observation brings energy and thread into relationship. That interaction shapes the condition of the thread in the next moment — and influences what possibilities remain available afterward.

This is an endless process of cause and effect unfolding across every available thread, in every moment. It is relatable to the butterfly effect: every thread its own butterfly, and every moment a flap of its wings.

At this point, a clarification is necessary.

When observation is spoken of here, it is not limited to human awareness, nor is it centered upon it. Observation is not a singular act performed by one species, nor is it synonymous with conscious intention as we commonly understand it. Humans participate in observation — but they are not its origin, and not its entirety.

Interaction occurs at every scale of existence: biological, environmental, systemic, and relational. Life responds to life. Systems respond to systems. Energy meets structure long before it is noticed by a human mind. Human awareness is simply one localized way this broader field of interaction becomes self-reflective.

This perspective does not place the construction of the present moment in human hands alone. It recognizes participation, not authorship — relationship, not command.

This perspective uses the word thread deliberately.

In the present moment, we only ever touch the leading edge — the tip. But if you were to trace that thread backward, you would find it woven from countless others: experiences, emotions, influences, and encounters layered across time.

Threads in the present are spun from fibers of the past.

Consciousness weaves threads together in the present moment — creating lived reality through an ongoing convergence of interaction.

Seen from the human perspective, this process scales outward.

The threads of an individual weave into family systems.

Families into communities.

Communities into cultures.

Cultures into civilizations.

Civilizations into planetary experience.

Together, they form the larger structure of living time.

The Present as a Junction, Not a Passage

From within the Living Time Perspective, the present moment is not a passage.

It is a junction.

A passage implies movement without participation — a conveyor belt carrying us forward regardless of how we engage.

A junction is different.

At a junction, many threads arrive at once:

Memory arrives.

Context arrives.

Emotion arrives.

Habit arrives.

Environment arrives.

Expectation arrives.

Possibility arrives.

Not sequentially.

Simultaneously.

But this convergence does not occur from a single direction, nor from a single point of view.

Each observer meets the present moment from a particular vantage point within the structure of time — carrying its own history, sensitivity, and field of view.

Within that local junction, threads arrive from all directions at once, shaped by scale, position, and relationship.

Other observers exist within that field — but to any given observer, they appear not as centers, but as threads themselves: entities to engage with, respond to, and be influenced by.

In this way, the present moment is not held by one observer, but completed through many.

A web of perception forms — layered, intersecting, distributed — through which the moment coheres as a shared reality.

This is why moments do not differ in significance by quantity alone.

Some moments redirect a life not because more happens, but because the configuration of threads — across observers, across scales — aligns in a way that allows a different continuation to emerge.

You have felt this before, even if you did not name it.

A sentence overheard at the right moment changes how you see a relationship.

A pause before responding alters the course of a conversation.

A familiar road taken on a difficult day leads somewhere new — not because the road changed, but because the field of engagement did.

Nothing dramatic is required.

No announcement is made.

And yet, the structure shifts.

Not every possible direction is taken.

Most continuations remain unrealized.

Some unfold without awareness.

A few are recognized just long enough to be entered.

The present moment is not where time passes through you.

It is where time takes shape — through a distributed, participatory unfolding.

The Illusion of Passage

To say that time passes suggests motion without structure — and without variation. It implies a uniform pace shared by all.

Lived experience contradicts this.

Some moments stretch — dense, heavy, slow.

Others vanish almost unnoticed.

This is not imagination. It is observation.

We synchronize our lives using shared tools — clocks, calendars, schedules — calibrated to Earth's motion around the sun. These tools are remarkably effective. They allow coordination across societies.

But they do not describe how time is experienced. Experience cannot be measured by the clock; when observation turns toward measurement, experience subtly reorganizes around it.

Strip away the clock.

Place two people in the same room, watching the same film.

One is absorbed — fully engaged, carried by the story.

The other is anxious — distracted by self-conscious thought, perhaps seated beside someone whose presence makes their heart flutter.

The film lasts the same number of minutes on the clock, but the experienced moment does not.

For one, time flies, lost in the brilliance of the film.

For the other, it drags, focused on their heartbeat and sweaty palms.

The clock remains unchanged.

The experience does not.

Which is why we cannot cleanly define the length of a moment. It varies from observer to observer.

Time and the Observer

This insight is not limited to psychology.

In Einstein's theory of relativity, time is not absolute. The rate at which it passes depends on the motion of the observer. A person traveling near the speed of light will experience time differently than someone at rest relative to Earth. This is known as time dilation.

From the traveler's perspective, time feels normal. Their body functions as usual. But compared to someone who remained behind, less time has passed for the traveler.

Once again, the observer matters.

You do not need to travel at the speed of light to recognize this effect. You only need to travel.

Jet lag is a familiar example. When you move east to west, the day stretches. When you move west to east, it compresses. Your body does not immediately agree with the clock. Sleep, hunger, alertness, and emotion fall out of sync. You are required to recalibrate — not just to a new schedule, but to a shared rhythm that differs from the one you carried with you.

I am not changing the scientific meaning of jet lag here. I am pointing to something relevant to this perspective:

The experience of time belongs first to the observer, not to the clock they adjust to.

Clocks synchronize society.

They do not synchronize experience.

They tell us when events occur.

They do not determine how moments resolve, are felt, or how they impact.

Time does not move at a universal rate from the inside.

Why "Now" Is Structurally Unique

Every moment may look similar on the surface, but the present holds a unique role.

The past is fixed.

The future remains as potentials.

Only the present allows interaction.

Only here can attention be directed.

Only here can meaning be assigned.

Only here can action be taken — or restraint chosen.

The present is not dramatic in appearance. It is often quiet. Ordinary. Easily overlooked.

But it is where consciousness and possibility meet.

From this junction, potentials transmute into fixed outcomes; the next moment takes shape — and the past is solidified into structure.

Yet none of this announces itself. There is no signal that a threshold has been crossed, no marker separating what was from what is becoming.

The present moment rarely signals its importance.

It does not arrive with emphasis or distinction.

It feels like now.

And yet, it is precisely this ordinariness that gives the present its power.

What shapes time most often does so without ceremony:

a word spoken or withheld,

a pause taken,

a habit repeated,

a thought believed or questioned.

Awareness and the Navigation of the Junction

To speak meaningfully about awareness, we must slow the scale.

We cannot relate to a near-infinite rate of moments per second. So here, awareness refers to the level of human-consciousness at which choice can be noticed — roughly the scale of seconds.

Awareness does not create more moments.

It does not necessarily interrupt the flow of time.

It changes how the junction is navigated and encountered.

Every present moment arrives already in motion. Threads enter the junction carrying momentum — shaped by history, habit, environment, emotion, and repetition. Much of this movement occurs beneath conscious notice.

Where awareness is minimal, that momentum tends to

resolve along paths of least resistance. Patterns continue forward — not because they are inevitable, but because they require no reinterpretation to proceed. The most established threads dominate, simply because they are already in motion.

This is true at every scale — individual and collective.

When awareness is present, something does not stop — but something loosens.

The moment becomes more legible.

Not only in what is visibly available to engage with, but in what is usually unseen: assumptions, emotional undercurrents, unspoken context, inherited meaning.

Threads once faint become perceptible.

Threads once automatic can be re-encountered rather than merely enacted.

A reaction that once dominated may still arise — but it no longer determines the junction by default.

Awareness does not command the moment. It adjusts the aperture through which it is met.

A comment can shift from insult to care.

An action can be understood in a wider context.

An outcome can be met with patience rather than reflex.

In this way, awareness does not decide what happens next

— but it broadens the range of how time is able to unfold.

Threads do not all carry the same vitality into the present moment.

Some arrive dense with momentum, others faint and easily overlooked.

Awareness does not command these threads, but it alters how energy engages them.

What is met with sustained attention may strengthen into a tangible thread — carried forward with its own momentum into future moments.

Likewise, awareness of misperception can loosen the momentum of a thread before it fully takes hold.

Paths that would have gone unnoticed remain available — not because they are forced into being, but because engagement redistributes what the moment can support.

The Present Is Not Owned by the Self

It is important to say this clearly:

The present moment does not belong to you.

You do not create it alone.

You do not control it.

Imagine a car approaching a highway interchange.

You choose your lane. You adjust your speed. But you

do not design the road, control the traffic, or dictate the conditions.

The present emerges from many trajectories intersecting at once — yours and others', human and non-human, personal and collective.

Your participation matters.

But it is not solitary.

Encounter, Not Command

From within the Living Time Perspective, the present moment is not something to be mastered.

It is something to be encountered.

You arrive with what you carry.

The world arrives with what it offers.

The junction forms.

What follows is shaped by relationship, not domination.

Living systems respond better to attentiveness than to force.

Chapter Ten

Consciousness Within Time

By now, we have established something essential.

Time, as explored in this perspective, is not merely a backdrop against which life unfolds. It is a living structure — one that grows, responds, and takes shape through interaction. We have examined its large-scale form, its branching patterns, and its smallest meaningful unit: the present moment.

What we have not yet examined directly is what moves within that structure.

Not as an object.

Not as a substance.

But as a presence.

Consciousness has been implicit in every chapter so far. It

has appeared in our discussions of observation, awareness, experience, and meaning. Yet it has remained deliberately undefined — because the moment we attempt to define consciousness too rigidly, we risk mistaking the tool for the thing itself.

Before we move forward, we need to acknowledge a quiet complication.

The word consciousness is used in many different ways, often without distinction.

Sometimes it refers to alertness or wakefulness.

Sometimes to personal identity or inner narration.

Sometimes to moral awareness.

Sometimes to subconscious processes beneath thought.

Sometimes to a collective or shared field of experience.

All of these uses are common. None of them are wrong. But they are not interchangeable.

When someone says consciousness, they may be referring to:

- immediate awareness — what is noticed right now
- psychological continuity — the sense of being "me" over time
- operational awareness — attention, focus, re-

sponsiveness

- background processing — habits, reflexes, emotional conditioning
- collective consciousness — shared meaning, culture, or field

In this chapter, we will not attempt to resolve these meanings into a single definition.

Instead, we will treat consciousness functionally, not absolutely.

Much as we speak of the nervous system without needing to explain the origin of life itself, we will speak of consciousness in terms of how it operates within time — not what it ultimately is.

To do this clearly, we will occasionally use gentle distinctions — not to divide consciousness into parts, but to help the reader track which aspect is being discussed at a given moment.

These distinctions are descriptive, not doctrinal.

They are guides, not claims.

Held rigidly, they will fail.

Held lightly, they will serve.

With that understanding in place, we can now ask the question that belongs here:

How does consciousness participate in the growth of time?

Consciousness Is Not a Thread

Within the Living Time Perspective, consciousness is not treated as a thread.

Threads are what consciousness engages with.

They are the forms, experiences, memories, objects, emotions, ideas, and conditions that appear within time.

Consciousness does not arise only from these forms, nor is it one among them. It is better understood as the capacity to engage — the faculty through which experience becomes possible at all.

We cannot observe consciousness directly in isolation.

What we observe instead is where it attaches:

- the continuity of experience it inhabits,
- the body it moves through,
- the history it carries forward.

This distinction matters.

When consciousness is mistakenly treated as an object — a thing among things — it becomes easy to confuse participation with control, and perspective with ownership.

So we set that aside.

Consciousness, in this view, is not a structure within time.

It is an active presence within the structure.

Consciousness as Continuity, Not Substance

Rather than imagining consciousness as a thing, it may be more helpful to understand it as continuity.

Not continuous awareness — which fluctuates —

but a continuous capacity for awareness, moving from moment to moment without division.

At the scale of lived experience, consciousness appears localized. Each person experiences themselves as distinct, bounded by a body and a history.

But from the scale of time itself, this separation softens.

Consciousness appears less like many isolated points and more like a field of engagement — expressing itself through countless local perspectives.

Every moment that has ever been experienced has been experienced by consciousness.

Every place where meaning has arisen has done so through it.

From within time, consciousness appears many.

From across time, it appears one.

This is not a claim of sameness.

It is a recognition of connection.

Separation is something experienced locally — not necessarily structured fundamentally.

The Nervous System of Time

To make this more tangible, consider a different metaphor.

Not threads branching through time —

but something closer to a nervous system.

In a living body, not all nerves are equal.

Some pathways carry immense volumes of information, integrating signals across the entire organism.

Others transmit faint, localized sensations — a change in pressure, a shift in temperature, a subtle signal at the surface.

But none are meaningless.

Each contributes.

Each informs the whole.

Together, they form a responsive network — continuously sensing, transmitting, adjusting.

Consciousness within time may function similarly.

Some experiences become central, shaping broad patterns and long-term structures.

Others remain peripheral — brief, localized, easily overlooked.

Some moments ripple outward with lasting consequence.

Others register quietly, then fade.

Yet all participate.

Information flows.

Feedback occurs.

Adjustment follows.

Nothing is entirely lost —

but not everything is equally emphasized.

To say that consciousness participates in time does not mean that any one perspective sits at the center of it.

There is no single observer at the axis of the present moment.

No privileged vantage point from which time is authored or directed.

The present moment is not owned by the self.

You do not create it alone.

You do not command it.

Instead, imagine the present moment as a point of convergence — not with a single observer standing above it, but with many observers surrounding it.

Each conscious being engages the same moment from a different position within the living structure of time.

Each brings a unique history, sensitivity, capacity, and angle of perception.

Seen this way, the present moment is encircled — not dominated — by awareness.

Individually, each perspective is partial.

Collectively, they form something closer to a whole.

No single observer contains the full picture.

But together, the many perspectives surrounding a moment allow it to be richly resolved — layered with meaning, context, response, and possibility.

This is why participation does not imply centrality.

And why humility belongs here.

Your awareness matters — not because it is singular, but because it contributes.

It joins countless other forms of awareness — human and non-human, biological and environmental, personal and collective — all engaging the same moment from different positions.

Each acts as an agent within the nervous system of time — a kind of nerve ending of consciousness — contributing its signal to a larger pattern from which lived reality takes shape.

To participate in time is not to dominate it.

It is to take responsibility for the quality of engagement you bring — knowing that what you notice, ignore, reinforce, or resist becomes part of a shared unfolding.

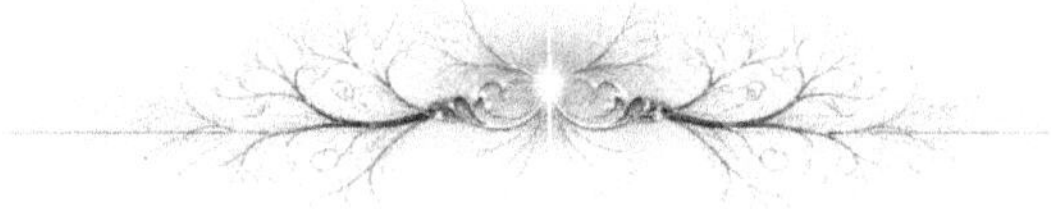

In a biological nervous system, not all components perform the same function, nor do they operate at the same scale. Some structures integrate signals across the entire body. Others operate locally, responding to immediate conditions with little awareness of the whole.

This does not create hierarchy of importance — only diversity of role. A localized reflex is no less essential than a centralized response. Without both, the system fails.

If consciousness functions as a nervous system within living time, it follows that agents of consciousness may also differ in range, resolution, and integration. Some participate in ways that ripple widely through the structure. Others engage more narrowly, shaping experience locally rather than globally.

From within a limited vantage point, this difference in scale can be misleading. Agents operating far from one's own position in the structure may appear opaque, repetitive, or indistinct — not because they lack experience, but because their orientation, function, or context lies beyond what can be readily perceived.

These distinctions do not imply lesser consciousness or diminished worth. They point instead to a distributed system in which awareness takes many forms, each necessary to the coherence of the whole. How these differences arise, and what they imply for the experience of identity and meaning, will be explored beyond the scope of this introduction.

Awareness as Interface

What distinguishes consciousness is not power, but interface.

Awareness is how consciousness meets time.

It is the point of contact where perception, attention, memory, and meaning converge.

When awareness is narrow, experience contracts.

When awareness widens, experience becomes more legible.

This does not mean that all possibilities suddenly become available. Living systems always operate within constraint.

But it does mean that more of what is already present can be seen, weighed, and responded to.

Awareness does not stop the movement of time.

It changes how the present junction is navigated.

A Vehicle Moving Through Time

At the scale of lived experience, it may help to set the tree aside and use a metaphor closer to daily life.

Imagine localized consciousness — your lived, moment-to-moment awareness — as a vehicle moving along a road.

The body is the vehicle itself. Its design, condition, and limits matter. They determine what terrain can be crossed, how fast you can travel, and how long the journey can continue in this particular form.

Localized consciousness sits in the driver's seat.

It faces forward.

All of the mirrors are angled for its perspective.

It perceives the road as it appears and responds to conditions, signals, obstacles, and openings as they arise.

From this position, it can feel as though the road simply exists — laid out in advance, fixed, given.

But this is only part of the picture.

The road is not built by the individual driver alone — yet it is not independent of consciousness either. What we call "the road" is shaped over time by collective participation: by countless observation points, interactions, decisions, repetitions, and meanings layered across moments.

Each engagement leaves a trace.

Each passage reinforces or alters the terrain that follows.

Your localized consciousness does not design the entire roadway — but it does participate in maintaining, wearing, shaping, and redirecting it. Navigation and construction are not separate processes here. They are different scales of the same activity.

The vehicle is not empty.

The ego is one such passenger — often insistent, often reactive, often convinced it knows the best route. It sits in the back seat, offering commentary, warnings, and demands. And while it does not belong at the wheel, it has learned how to reach forward and tug at it.

Awareness determines the grip consciousness has of the wheel, the field of view through the windshield and perception through the mirrors.

But the vehicle carries more than passengers.

It also carries cargo.

With every engagement of a thread — every interaction with another conscious being, every moment that enters experience — something is taken in. Not a replica of the encounter, but a fractal of it: a compressed imprint of relationship, meaning, emotion, and response.

Some of these imprints remain vivid and easily accessible. Others recede into subtle influence. But each interaction leaves its mark, and the collection continues to grow; fibers spun into the thread, giving more structure, character, and thickness.

Experience is not left behind as we move forward.

It is carried — folded into the vehicle itself — influencing how perception, reaction, and choice arise in moments that follow.

Within the Living Time Perspective, this accumulated cargo becomes part of the weave. It is not static memory, but living structure — a thread acknowledged early, even if examined more fully later.

The road itself is shared.

Other vehicles travel alongside you — sometimes briefly, sometimes for long stretches. Some move faster. Some slower. Some change lanes abruptly. Some exit without warning.

You may travel near another for a time, but never for the same reason. Never toward the same destination. Never carrying the same cargo of memory, history, and intention.

Along the way, experiences accumulate — not as souvenirs, but as patterns of engagement. What is carried forward is not the whole of what was encountered, but a fractal of it — shaped by attention, emotion, repetition, and meaning. From every interaction, only certain aspects are taken up, reinforced, or integrated. The rest passes through without taking root.

Each encounter leaves a trace:

- a lesson learned,
- a sensitivity sharpened,
- a reflex formed,
- a pattern strengthened or softened.

There is always a fractal transferred and carried forward.

These traces do not dictate the journey.

But they influence how it unfolds.

Seen this way, participation in time is not about command.

It is about shared construction through navigation.

And navigation, practiced with awareness, changes not only where you go — but how the road itself continues to take shape.

Chapter Eleven

The Weaver

By now, something may feel quietly different.

Not because you have been given answers, but because familiar ones may no longer fit as neatly as they once did.

We have spoken about time as a living structure — something that grows, branches, responds, and remembers.

We have looked at the present moment not as a passage, but as a junction.

We have examined consciousness not as a thing, but as a presence — a continuity that moves within time without being contained by it.

In doing so, we have gently loosened many of the assumptions that usually hold the self in place.

You are not simply your body.

You are not the voice of your thoughts.

You are not the sum of your memories, nor the shape of your fears.

You are not consciousness as a whole —

and you are not separate from it either.

When these familiar anchors fall away, an old question often returns:

Who am I?

This chapter does not attempt to answer that question.

Instead, it offers a way of standing within the question.

Not an Identity, but a Role

There is a difference between what something is and how it participates.

Much of human struggle arises from confusing function with essence — from turning what we do into what we are, or mistaking roles for certainty. Living systems rarely operate this way. They move through roles, relationships, and processes that shift with context and time.

From within the Living Time Perspective, we speak of a role that encompasses what maintains the body, carries the ego, and participates consciously in the growth of time.

This role operates primarily at the scale of the present moment — working with available threads to form the tapestry of lived and recorded experience.

We name this role the Weaver.

Not because the name is definitive, but because it points toward function rather than essence.

If another word serves you better, you are free to use it.

The name is not what matters.

The role is.

The Weaver is not an identity to claim.

It is a role you may recognize yourself inhabiting.

To see yourself as a Weaver is not to say, "This is what I am."

It is to say, "This is how I participate."

A Weaver is not the fabric.

A Weaver is not the loom.

A Weaver is not the pattern as a whole.

A Weaver is one who works with what is available — who selects, combines, responds, and participates in what takes shape.

The degree of participation rests within the freedom of the Weaver.

You may apply as much or as little awareness as you choose in any given moment and still participate in the weaving of time.

You may move alongside another Weaver for a while, shaped by shared conditions and overlapping threads. Together you can co-create a part of the whole. But it is important to understand this clearly:

You will never be able to see it in the same way as another.

Your experience will never be the same unfolding branch.

It will always be uniquely yours.

And it will always matter just as much as any other.

Every path contributes — not by repeating what is known, but by revealing what could not appear any other way.

Consciousness as Agent, Not Owner

Earlier in this introduction, we made an important distinction: Consciousness is not a thread within time. It is the presence that engages threads.

Here, we refine that distinction.

When we speak of consciousness, we are not referring only to the localized sense of self — the voice behind the eyes, the stream of thought, the feeling of "me" moving through the day. That is one expression of consciousness, but it is not the whole of it.

Consciousness, as explored here, is broader than any single viewpoint — and yet it only encounters time through viewpoints, like light shaped by the form it passes through.

It does not experience time all at once. It experiences time through participation.

Each localized perspective — human or otherwise — offers a particular angle of engagement: shaped by a body, conditioned by history, constrained by circumstance, and situated within a specific present moment. Through these countless localized engagements, consciousness encounters contrast, tension, novelty, and depth.

This is where the Weaver belongs.

The Weaver is not consciousness itself. The Weaver is an element of consciousness acting locally.

An agent through which experience is gathered.

At the scale of lived experience, the Weaver is the interface — the point where awareness meets the present junction and engages available threads. Through attention, response, repetition, and restraint, the Weaver participates in what takes shape next.

In this sense, the Weaver functions much like a nerve ending within a larger nervous system.

Each Weaver perceives from a unique position. Each registers different signals. Each transmits a partial picture.

No single Weaver holds the whole. But together, these countless localized perspectives allow consciousness to sense itself across time — to register pattern, relationship, and change.

This does not confer ownership. The present moment is not yours to command. Time does not belong to the self.

But participation is real.

Every act of observation sends information into the larger structure. Every moment engaged contributes to how the weave continues.

This is not power in the sense of control. It is responsibility in the sense of relationship.

To recognize yourself as a Weaver is not to elevate the self. It is to understand your position.

You are not separate from the movement of time. You are one of the ways its experience is gathered.

Why This Is Not Always Gentle

This understanding can feel unsettling — not emotionally, but structurally.

If time grows through interaction, and consciousness encounters it through experience, then no single quality can define how that growth unfolds. Interaction does not arrive filtered for comfort. It arrives as it is — shaped by contrast, interruption, alignment, friction, and change.

Questions about difficulty, loss, and hardship have followed human reflection across every culture and era. They do not arise because something has gone wrong in understanding, but because disruption is a visible feature of lived systems. Wherever there is movement, there is variation. Wherever there is variation, there is unevenness in how experience unfolds.

This perspective does not ask why hardship exists.

It does not assign purpose to pain.

It does not attempt to reconcile suffering into meaning.

Instead, it places difficulty where it can be observed: within the dynamics of interaction itself.

Living systems do not develop through repetition alone. If every encounter mirrored the last, structure would remain thin, predictable, and limited in range. What alters structure is not uniformity, but difference — moments that interrupt expectation, challenge orientation, or introduce conditions that cannot be met automatically.

Contrast sharpens perception.

Tension exposes limits.

Interruption reveals dependency.

These are not virtues. They are conditions.

From within the Living Time Perspective, time is not organized to preserve ease. It is organized to register experience. And experience, by its nature, includes a full spectrum of conditions — some fluid, some resistant, some coherent, some destabilizing.

This does not make hardship beneficial.

It does not excuse harm.

It does not sanctify injustice.

Those distinctions matter, and they are not blurred here.

What is being described is not the value of suffering, but its position within a living process. In complex systems, not every interaction is balanced. Not every outcome is fair. Not every moment reveals its significance while it is occurring.

And yet, each encounter — whether marked by ease or resistance — alters what follows. It leaves a trace. It changes orientation. It reshapes what becomes possible next.

This is not a moral conclusion.

It is a structural one.

It does not ask the reader to reinterpret their past, nor to extract meaning where none is felt. It simply recognizes that time grows through interaction — and interaction includes the full range of conditions life presents.

The Weaver Within Constraint

A Weaver does not create from nothing.

They work with what is already there.

Threads arrive conditioned — by history, environment, capacity, and momentum. Some are thick with repetition. Others are faint and easily overlooked. Some pull insistently. Others wait quietly at the edge of awareness.

The Weaver does not command these threads.

They relate to them.

They choose where to place attention.

They decide how long to hold a pattern.

They sense when to tighten, when to release, and when to let something unravel.

Often, this happens unconsciously.

Habit weaves.

Fear weaves.

The ego weaves — clumsily, loudly, always convinced it knows the pattern that will finally bring safety.

But awareness changes the quality of participation.

With awareness, the Weaver begins to see not just what is happening, but how it is happening.

This does not eliminate pain.

It does not grant immunity.

It does not ensure wisdom in every moment.

But it introduces choice where there was once only momentum.

Momentum does not disappear — but it is no longer the only force at work.

You Are One of the Ways It Happens

This may be the most important point in this chapter.

You are not the center of time.

But you are one of the ways time continues.

Your experiences are not generic.

Your position is not interchangeable.

The way you encounter moments — the way you respond, resist, notice, or withdraw — is unique, and can never be fully shared by another Weaver.

Words can only point.

They can never be.

No one else occupies your exact position within the living structure of time.

No one else brings your particular history, sensitivity, and capacity into this moment.

This does not make you special in the sense of elevation.

It makes you irreplaceable in the sense of contribution.

Your thread is never fully shared.

Never fully replicated.

And yet, it becomes part of a larger tapestry — influencing patterns you may never see directly.

Time does not wait for your understanding — but it does pass through your participation.

A Quiet Invitation

To recognize yourself as a Weaver is not to claim authority over reality.

It is to accept participation within it.

It is to understand that moments are not simply endured or escaped — they are met.

And how they are met matters.

Not in some cosmic accounting sense.

But in the way patterns form.

In the way habits soften or harden.

In the way meaning accumulates or dissolves over time.

This chapter does not ask you to adopt a new identity.

It offers a lens — one you may return to, or set aside, as needed.

If you find it useful, it will not be because it explains everything, but because it gives you a place to stand and observe a much larger picture.

It will be because, at some later moment, you recognize yourself standing at a junction — and realize you have more relationship to that moment than you once believed.

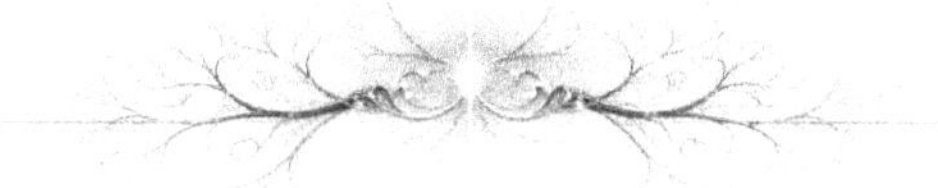

To see yourself as a Weaver is not to claim authority over time, but to acknowledge participation within it. Every moment already involves you. Awareness does not introduce agency — it refines it.

What comes next is not about belief.

It is about learning the craft.

As with any living art, skill develops through attention, patience, and practice. Over time, a Weaver begins to sense tension before it snaps, flow before it accelerates, imbalance before it hardens into structure. Intention grows quieter. Responsiveness grows sharper.

Participation becomes more deliberate — not forceful, but skillful.

And with that skill, the structure that emerges carries a different quality. Not because it is controlled, but because it is tended. Not because outcomes are guaranteed, but because engagement becomes conscious.

This perspective does not promise mastery of time.

It invites familiarity with the act of weaving — and with the quiet responsibility that comes from knowing your hands are already at the loom.

Chapter Twelve

Why This Perspective Exists

Nothing in this perspective has changed time itself.

Time does not require a new explanation. It does not wait for our understanding. It continues—patient, layered, alive—whether we notice it or not.

So a reasonable question arises:

Why look at time this way at all?

For me, the answer has always come from a particular kind of curiosity. Not the passing kind, but the persistent one. The kind that needs coherence. The kind that looks for logic not as reduction, but as relationship. The kind that cannot separate meaning from experience, or experience from structure.

I have always needed life to make sense—not in a tidy or comforting way, but in a way that holds together when examined closely. When something mattered to me, I needed to understand how it worked, why it behaved as it did, and where I stood within it. Meaning, for me, was never abstract. It was something to be lived.

That impulse shaped how I moved through the world. I became a reader. A listener. A collector of ideas. I explored philosophy, spiritual teachings, scientific frameworks, and personal accounts of transformation. Certain ideas resonated immediately—I AM among them. They carried a truth that bypassed argument and landed directly in experience.

And yet, I struggled to remain inside those insights.

They arrived as moments—clear, powerful, fleeting—but I could not sustain them. There was no structure I could step into. No way to engage them without either flattening them into belief or letting them drift back into abstraction. The insight was present, but the relationship was missing.

The same was true of manifestation. The patterns aligned. The concepts made sense. But without a framework grounded in lived experience, they remained unstable—either oversimplified or over-mystified, depending on the lens applied.

The Living Time Perspective did not arrive as an answer.

It arrived as a way of holding questions without losing

coherence.

It offered me a structure that could accommodate mystery without surrendering logic, and agency without claiming control. A way of relating to time that felt practical without becoming mechanical. A way of engaging meaning without demanding certainty.

From this perspective, I no longer feel as though I am standing outside experience, hoping to influence it from a distance. I feel present within it.

As a Weaver, I can enter the moment deliberately. I can recognize the threads already here. I can sense which ones are thick with momentum, which are fragile, which are asking for attention, and which are ready to be released. I can work—not to dictate outcomes or escape uncertainty—but to participate honestly in the growth of time as it moves through me.

This perspective does not make the unseen mystical.

It makes it relational.

It does not promise control.

It invites readiness.

And perhaps most importantly, it has helped me find logic and answers to questions I have carried since I was very young.

Questions surrounding death were among the earliest philosophical questions I asked—and answered—within myself.

I don't remember when the focus shifted from fearing what came next to fearing what I might leave behind. But at some point, that fear became clear and directional. What troubled me was not the end of experience, but the possibility of being forgotten—of passing through without leaving a meaningful trace.

Even then, I sensed that impact mattered. Not in monuments or recognition, but in the way I treated others, the care I showed, the integrity I held, and the wake I left behind as I moved through the world. That question quietly shaped the kind of person I grew into.

Looking back now, I recognize this as an early intuition of the same truth this perspective points toward:

What endures is not the body. Not the ego. Not the story we tell about ourselves, or the objects we collect along the way.

What endures is the weave. The threads we touch. The moments we shape. The subtle ways our presence alters the structure of time for others—even briefly.

This framework exists to offer a lens for seeing that participation more clearly.

It does not teach you how to live. It does not provide answers to questions only you can resolve. It does not ask for belief.

It offers orientation.

If you choose to set it down here, nothing is lost.

If you carry it forward, it may surface quietly—in how you notice moments, how you respond to difficulty, how you relate to the future without grasping for it.

From within this perspective, wonder is no longer a rare lightning strike. It becomes a steady condition.

Sonder stops being a sudden rupture — that jolt of realizing everyone else has a life as complex as yours — and becomes something gentler, almost ordinary. A background awareness. A quiet companionship with the fact that meaning is everywhere because participation is everywhere.

Future works may explore this perspective more deeply — and more personally. This book provides the foundation. What follows will reflect where my own journey leads after having released it.

I am still discovering what this perspective will become — and I am okay with that.

For now, this book stops here.

Leaving you with a simple recognition until we work together again:

You are already participating. You always have been. Time is growing through you—quietly, patiently—one junction at a time.

A Continuing Thread

If this lens resonated with you — if it shifted something, clarified something, unsettled something in a useful way — I would welcome your reflection.

Not as praise.

Not as agreement.

But as participation.

Every review, every thoughtful response, becomes another thread in the weave of this work.

It helps this perspective reach the hands of others who may be asking similar questions.

If you feel moved to share how this book met you — what it stirred, what it challenged, what it illuminated — your words will help shape where it grows next.

The conversation does not end here.

It continues wherever attention meets it.

Thank you for the way you engaged these pages.

That alone has already altered the structure.

Amazon.com: https://a.co/d/040y6oro

Notes on Language

The words used throughout this introduction are tools, not containers.

They are chosen for how they point, not for how tightly they define.

What follows is not a glossary in the traditional sense, but a set of working notes — offered only to help you carry the lens forward without mistaking the language for the thing itself.

If any term here feels limiting, replace it.

If another word serves you better, use it.

The perspective does not depend on the vocabulary, but on a willingness to observe more openly.

Awareness

Used here to describe the capacity to notice — particularly at the scale where choice becomes visible. Awareness refers to the field or interface within which experience can be perceived, interpreted, and engaged. It describes the range of legibility available in a moment: how much of what is present can be noticed, held, and meaningfully related to.

Awareness is not constant, nor is it required for experience to occur. Moments unfold regardless. What awareness alters is not whether something happens, but how much of what is happening can be seen and weighed. In this sense, awareness shapes the width of contact with the present, within which observation may occur.

Consciousness

Not treated as an object, substance, or possession. In this work, consciousness is approached functionally — as the capacity for experience and engagement within time, expressed through localized viewpoints. It is discussed in terms of how it participates and relates, not what it ultimately is.

Junction

Refers to the present moment as a meeting point rather than a passage. A junction is where multiple threads arrive simultaneously — memory, context, emotion, environment, habit, possibility — and enter into relationship. The term emphasizes convergence without implying control.

Meaning

Not something found, but something formed. Meaning arises through interaction — between experience, memory, emotion, interpretation, and time. It is woven, not uncovered, and remains fluid across scale and perspective.

Observation

Used here to describe engagement rather than passive witnessing. Observation refers to the act or event of contact within the field of awareness — the moment where interaction occurs and experience takes shape. It is the point at which what is available becomes actual, where ambiguity resolves into lived experience.

Observation includes attention, interaction, and responsiveness, and often operates below conscious awareness. It precedes explanation and interpretation. In this perspective, observation is not separate from structure-building; it is the movement within awareness through which moments are formed and the continuity of time is shaped.

Pattern

Refers to recurring structures of relationship, not repeated events. Patterns may appear across scales — personal, cultural, biological, cosmic — without being identical. Recognizing a pattern does not imply inevitability; it offers orientation.

Present Moment

Not treated as a thin slice of time passing by, but as the only location where interaction occurs. The present is where threads meet, where attention can be directed, and where the next moment takes shape. Its "length" is deliberately left undefined.

Thread

Used to describe anything consciousness can engage with — experiences, objects, thoughts, emotions, memories, expectations, ideas. A thread carries history and momentum. The term emphasizes continuity and relationship rather than isolation.

Time

Not approached as a neutral container or a simple line. From this perspective, time is explored as a living structure — something that grows, branches, thickens, and responds. This is a perspective, not a claim of physical fact.

Weaver

Names a role, not an identity. The weaver refers to localized consciousness participating in the present moment — engaging available threads through attention, response, and restraint. The term points to function rather than essence.

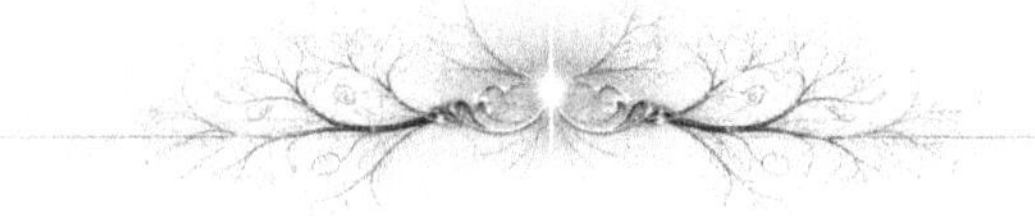

These notes are offered as gentle landmarks, nothing more.

They are meant to reduce confusion, not resolve ambiguity.

If, as you move forward, the language begins to feel transparent — if the words fall away and the relationships remain — then they have done their work.

A Note on the Author

Some readers may recognize familiar questions here — not because this perspective appears elsewhere, but because the curiosity that shaped it has been moving for a long time.

J.W. Pressler's first novel, *The Shift: Discovering Inner Evolution*, explored that curiosity through fiction — circling themes of inner change, ancient wisdom, and unseen connection without yet naming their structure. While working on its sequel, *Echoes of As Above*, questions of time emerged that needed to be understood before the story could continue. The perspective developed in this work is the result of that pause.

For those who wish to explore these questions with the freedom that fiction allows, The Shift and more can be found here:

Yjpresspublishing.com

www.ingramcontent.com/pod-product-compliance
Lightning Source LLC
LaVergne TN
LVHW010949110826
845149LV00015B/3280

* 9 7 9 8 9 9 8 6 5 9 6 2 1 *